# 150 Nature Hot Spots in
# CANADA

# 150 Nature Hot Spots in CANADA

## The Best Parks, Conservation Areas and Wild Places

Selected and edited by Debbie Olsen

FIREFLY BOOKS

# A FIREFLY BOOK

Published by Firefly Books Ltd. 2020

First printing

**Library of Congress Control Number:** 2019953048

**Library and Archives Canada Cataloguing in Publication**

Title: 150 nature hot spots in Canada : the best parks, conservation areas
    and wild places / selected and edited by Debbie Olsen.

Other titles: One hundred and fifty nature hot spots in Canada

Names: Olsen, Debbie, 1965- author.

Description: Includes index.

Identifiers: Canadiana 20190218460 | ISBN 9780228102427 (softcover)

Subjects: LCSH: Natural areas—Canada—Guidebooks. | LCSH: Parks—Canada—Guidebooks. |
    LCSH: Protected areas—Canada—Guidebooks. | LCSH: Wilderness areas—Canada—Guidebooks. |
    LCSH: Canada—Description and travel. | LCSH: Canada—Guidebooks. | LCGFT: Guidebooks.

Classification: LCC FC76 .O47 2020 | DDC 971.07/4—dc23

Published in the United States by
Firefly Books (U.S.) Inc.
P.O. Box 1338, Ellicott Station
Buffalo, New York 14205

Published in Canada by
Firefly Books Ltd.
50 Staples Avenue, Unit 1
Richmond Hill, Ontario L4B 0A7

Cover design: Noor Majeed
Interior design: Stacey Cho

Printed in Korea

 We acknowledge the financial support
of the Government of Canada.

# Dedication:

To Greg Olsen, my favourite photographer and travelling companion. And to our children, Kolby, Brady and Carleigh, Dylan and Caitlyn, and Kelsey. I feel at home in nature but never more so than when my family is with me. Thanks for the hikes, camping trips and outdoor adventures.

– D.O.

# Contents

# Introduction

Canada is a country of outstanding natural beauty, and the proof is in the numbers. At almost 10 million square kilometres, it is the second-largest country in the world by total area. It stretches east to west from the Atlantic Ocean to the Pacific Ocean and northward to the Arctic Ocean, encompassing 20 ecozones and 194 different ecoregions. Canada's lakes, rivers, streams and wetlands hold 20 per cent of the world's fresh water, and yet Canada's human population amounts to only a half of one per cent of the world's total. Canada is home to the Rocky Mountains, the Great Lakes, the world's longest recreational trail and a long list of UNESCO World Heritage Sites. Simply put, there's a lot of wilderness, wildlife and wide-open space.

There is beauty to be found in every region of Canada, and the biggest challenge in creating a book about Canada's nature hot spots was narrowing the list down to just 150 places. As a result, the list contained here is by no means comprehensive. Many exceptional sites could not be included in this edition. After extensive consultation, the final list comprises well-known nature hot spots that are popular with locals and visitors as well as lesser-known sites that are true hidden gems. The hot spots are organized by region, moving generally from west to east.

There are many ways to enjoy nature, and the special interest section covers some of them. Information about multi-day backpacking and cycling trails, aurora viewing, scenic drives, wildlife watching, birding and unusual nature hot spots can be found in this section.

Be safety conscious when you go out exploring. There are many hazards in natural areas, and a little advance preparation will ensure your visit goes well. Visit the destination website or call to confirm a particular park or park feature is open. Make sure you have water, food, and adequate clothing and gear for the activities you plan to enjoy. You will need to pack bear spray if you're hiking or cycling in bear country. In polar bear country, you may need to hire a bear guard. It's always safer to hike in a group than to hike alone, and it's important to let someone know where you're going — especially if the destination is remote. If you're driving to a remote spot, make sure your car is in good working order and that you have a spare tire and know how to change it — some remote areas of the country do not have cellphone service.

## Icon Legend

These icons appear throughout to give you an idea of the available activities and features at each hot spot.

 **Wildlife viewing**

 **Hiking**

 **Camping**

 **Cycling**

 **Horseback riding**

 **Rock/Ice Climbing**

 **Paddling**

 **Swimming**

 **Scuba diving or snorkelling**

 **Fishing**

 **Power boating**

 **Sailing**

 **Surfing**

 **Cross-country skiing**

 **Snowshoeing**

 **Stargazing**

Fossil hunting

↑ Editor and writer Debbie Olsen takes in the spectacular views along the Chilkoot Trail, which runs from Alaska, USA, to British Columbia.

## Accessibility

Information regarding universal access has been taken from available data provided by each location. Please note that this data may refer to specific trails, parking or toilets at the hot spot, and visitors with accessibility needs may be unable to fully experience the highlights we profile. Please confirm the availability of accessible facilities and trails prior to departure.

When in nature, remember that you're a guest in a place inhabited by many other species. Stay on prescribed trails to avoid damaging fragile flora that might be growing along the edge of the trail. Keep a safe distance away from wildlife. Never feed wild animals. And lastly, respect other outdoor enthusiasts and the wildlife that make the land their home by leaving no trace of your visit behind.

Canada's wild places and wildlife are the country's greatest treasures. Never has it been more important to understand and appreciate nature. Wildlife and natural areas are under threat. Climate change, pollution, decreasing biodiversity, habitat loss, introduced species and unsustainable practices are changing the world,

## Nature Hot Spots and Dogs

Given the delicate nature of parks and natural areas, some sites do not allow visitors to bring dogs. Other sites that do allow dogs may restrict them to certain trails and areas. In most cases, these restrictions are designed to protect sensitive ecosystems and wildlife. If you plan to bring your dog, please contact the destination in advance to learn about limitations and any precautions you must take. Please obey all signs, keep your dog on a leash, dispose of your pet's excrement appropriately and take additional care around wildlife and when meeting other people and pets.

but we can do better. The first step is to connect with nature.

I believe that nature can heal your soul, and I also believe that one soul inspired can help to heal the world. We can all do something to make the world a better place. I sincerely hope you will enjoy this book and use it for years to come to help you discover new hot spots to visit and new ways to connect with nature.

USA

British Columbia

Prince George

Pacific Ocean

Kamloops

Vancouver
Nanaimo

Chilliwack
Abbotsford

Victoria

16

16

16

13

14

11

1

6

7

5

3

2

4

1

1

1

10

# West Coast

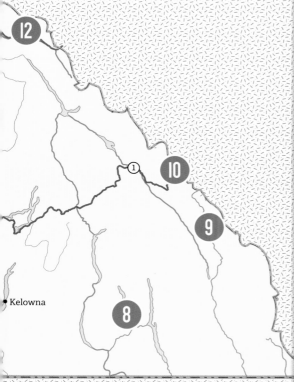

Alberta

12

①

10

9

• Kelowna

8

USA

## British Columbia

JUAN DE FUCA PROVINCIAL PARK

# Botanical Beach

by Lyndsay Fraser

*This shoreline's remarkably diverse intertidal life provides an opportunity to witness some of BC's most fascinating marine fauna first-hand*

## What Makes This Hot Spot Hot?

- Tidal pools are home to extremely diverse varieties of species.
- To reach the beaches, visitors can walk a beautiful temperate rainforest trail loop, which also connects to the Juan de Fuca Trail.
- There are opportunities to see marine mammals, such as orcas, grey whales, seals, sea lions and otters.

**Address:** Juan de Fuca Provincial Park, off of West Coast Rd (Hwy 14) near Port Renfrew, BC
**GPS:** 48.534075; –124.443427
**Tel.:** (250) 474-1336
**Website:** www.env.gov
.bc.ca/bcparks/explore
/parkpgs/juan_de_fuca
/trailhd.html#botanical

**Open year-round**

↗ **These purple sea urchins use their sharp spines to grind out shallow cavities into the sandstone, creating places where they can reside at low tide.**

A short walk through coastal temperate rainforest, a beautiful experience in itself, will bring you to the perfect spot to experience the diverse marine life of the Pacific Northwest. Protected within the boundaries of Juan de Fuca Provincial Park, Botanical Beach is the ideal spot for exploring the rich intertidal zone, the area that lies between the highest and lowest tides.

Botanical Beach is home to an abundance of life, so expect to see multiple species of crabs, snails, sea anemones, limpets, barnacles, sea urchins, mussels, chitons, sea stars and brittle stars, as well as the occasional nudibranch or sea cucumber. The crystal-clear tidal pools allow for perfect viewing, but take the time to carefully examine each one — you will be surprised at what comes to life. An unassuming snail shell may be home to one of several species of hermit crab, and giant green anemones may be seen using their stinging tentacles to catch a meal.

The marine life is fragile and the rocks can be very slippery,

↑ The fascinating geology of this park has created unique viewing opportunities, as the sandstone has been carved away by wave-tossed rocks and boulders that have ground uniquely smooth and deep pools into the shoreline.

so step thoughtfully — delicate snails, limpets, barnacles and other amazing creatures inhabit most surfaces, carefully enclosed in their shells to avoid desiccating while waiting for the tide to return. Plan your trip with the tides in mind, arriving at least an hour before low tide for time to explore the entire stretch of this family-friendly shoreline. The parking lot of this popular spot fills up quickly, so arriving early in the morning is best.

Botany Bay, an adjacent beach accessible from the same trail loop, is also worth a visit for beautiful views of rugged cliffs and the black basalt shoreline. While the intertidal life is well worth the trip on all but the coldest days of the year, the area also offers opportunities for large marine mammal sightings — California and northern sea lions can be seen during the summer months, and harbour seals and river otters are also frequently spotted in the area. It is not uncommon for these shores to be visited by orcas or even grey whales as they migrate north up the coast between March and April.

## PACIFIC RIM NATIONAL PARK RESERVE

# Broken Group Islands

by Christina Smyth

### *This archipelago within a national park protects an ocean paradise*

## What Makes This Hot Spot Hot?

- These unique islands feature white sand beaches, rocky shores and tidal pools.
- This is the birthplace of the Tseshaht First Nation, and you can discover many cultural objects.
- Ocean currents create a late-summer bloom of micro-organisms that turn the water bioluminescent.

**Address:** Main Access via Ucluelet, BC
**GPS:** 48.91905; –125.28001
**Tel.:** (250) 726-3500
**Website:** www.pc.gc.ca /en/pn-np/bc/pacificrim /activ/visit4c/activ4

**Open year-round; July and August are the best times to visit**

↗ **The shell of a moon snail.**

The Broken Group Islands are an archipelago of over 100 islands with white sand beaches, rocky shores, a rich Indigenous history and many opportunities for wildlife viewing. Visitors frequently spot seals, sea lions, grey whales and a variety of other ocean mammals. However, the biodiversity of these islands is most notably demonstrated in the intertidal zone, by the marine invertebrates that inhabit these waters.

On Wouwer Island you will find the Great Tide Pool, which is large enough to swim in and filled with many ocean animals, including sea cucumbers, sea stars and moon snails. Visit at low tide for the best opportunity to get up close and personal with these creatures. If you are feeling ambitious and wish to take a dip, bring a wetsuit and a snorkel, as the water is cold year-round.

The summer months bring an abundance of bioluminescent micro-organisms called diatoms. When disturbed, these diatoms emit a burst of blue-white light. After the sun sets, run your hand through the water and watch it glow behind you. If you are lucky, you may see a school of fish creating a moving ball of light beneath the ocean surface.

Plan your visit in mid-August for the best chance of experiencing this natural wonder.

The Broken Group Islands are situated within the Pacific Rim National Park Reserve. Beach keepers maintain the area and have a wealth of information to share with visitors. They may be able to point you toward culturally significant areas of the Tseshaht First Nation, to whom this archipelago is of great importance. Benson Island, the birthplace of the Tseshaht, has an interpretive display featuring a traditionally carved house post. A guided kayak tour from Ucluelet is the easiest way to access these islands. For experienced kayakers, another option is to rent a water taxi to carry kayaks to the islands and then explore the archipelago on your own.

## PACIFIC RIM NATIONAL PARK RESERVE

# Long Beach

by Christina Smyth

### *This long, sandy beach may have you exploring the seashore for days*

## What Makes This Hot Spot Hot?

- Peering into tidal pools reveals sea stars, anemones and other interesting intertidal organisms.
- Migrating grey whales are frequently sighted in the spring on their way north from Mexico.
- Trails through the forest behind the beach offer interpretive signs and glimpses of the ocean between large trees.

**Address:** Pacific Rim National Park Reserve, 485 Wick Rd, Ucluelet, BC
**GPS:** 49.06758; –125.74935
**Tel.:** (250) 726-3500
**Websites:** www.pc.gc.ca/en/pn -np/bc/pacificrim/index and www.longbeachmaps.com

**Open year-round**

&#x1F50D; &#x1F6B6; &#x26FA; &#x1F6B2; &#x1F3CA; &#x1F3A3;

&#x267F; (Check ahead)

This long, sandy beach, spanning 16 kilometres along the west coast of Vancouver Island, is one of the earliest recorded surfing beaches in British Columbia. It is divided into three areas: Wikaninnish, Combers and Incinerator Rock. The seashore and surrounding forests offer many opportunities for exploration by naturalists.

From Combers Beach you can view Sea Lion Rock, a nesting haven for seabirds and a popular area for sea lions to hang out. If you are particularly interested in birds, loiter in the estuary at Combers Beach, where the river leaves the forest and enters the ocean. A mixture of salt and fresh water creates a nutrient-rich habitat, attracting birds. Trumpeter swans are known to frequent this area.

↗ **Surfers are a common sight amid the waves at Long Beach.**

Migrating grey whales return from Mexico to the Pacific Northwest in the spring; stroll the beach in March for the best chance to see one. Other cetaceans you may spot include humpback whales, orcas and a variety of porpoises.

Hollows in rocky outcroppings create sanctuaries at low tide for sea stars, anemones and the occasional small fish. Safe from marine predators, these critters are trapped in these small tidal pools until the ocean rises again to cover them. Organisms that have adapted to live in tidal pools are unique and hardy. They must be able to survive a wide range of temperatures and adjust to lowered oxygen levels as the sun heats the water and animals in the pools produce waste.

On Wick Road, at the southern end of the beach, you will find the Kwisitis Visitor Centre. Interpretive displays provide information about the natural history of the area and the Nuu-chah-nulth Nations. From here, access trails through the forest, which can provide a welcome respite from a hot day on the beach. You may see signs warning of dangerous riptides in the area, and swimming is not recommended in many places along this beach.

↑ **Humpback whales are frequently sighted from shore and sea.**

↓ **Sea stars, like this ochre sea star, feed on barnacles and mussels.**

## MACMILLAN PROVINCIAL PARK

# Cathedral Grove

by Lyndsay Fraser

**_While some trees remain standing, other fallen giants provide food and shelter for the diverse flora and fauna of Cathedral Grove_**

### What Makes This Hot Spot Hot?

- Easily accessed trails wind through groves of giant trees.
- The park contains imposing 800-year-old Douglas firs and western red cedars.
- Nurse logs provide nutrients and habitats for countless organisms.

**Address:** MacMillan Provincial Park, Alberni Hwy (Hwy 4), Port Alberni, BC
**GPS:** 49.2876; –124.66648
**Tel.:** (250) 474-1336
**Website:** www.env.gov
.bc.ca/bcparks/explore
/parkpgs/macmillan

**Open year-round**

&#x267f; (Check ahead)

An entire community of mosses and lichens inhabits the trunks of these massive trees.

Cathedral Grove, found in MacMillan Provincial Park, may be the most famous old-growth forest in British Columbia, and for good reason. Douglas firs and western red cedars, some over 800 years old, tower over their awestruck admirers. Most of the province's biggest stands of Douglas fir of this maturity are difficult to access or, sadly, still being logged for timber, but this stand is thankfully very easy to reach. Despite its large number of annual visitors, this forest remains a treasure trove of natural wonders worth visiting.

In 1997 a severe windstorm swept through the park, and hundreds of these ancient trees fell. Although this storm severly damaged the trail system (some of the trails were never reopened), the ecosystem itself continues to thrive. The massive fallen trees maintain a vital role, even in their death. Sunlight, able to reach the forest floor once again, stimulates new growth in an understorey that had been largely deprived of the sun's rays for hundreds of

→ **Phenomenal giant Douglas firs, up to 9 metres around, are protected within the boundaries of the park.**

years. The stumps and logs of these fallen trees act as a nursery for new growth, providing nutrients and ideal conditions for the next generation of plants, which sprout and take root on their decaying bodies. Nurse logs have become home to a diverse assortment of fungi, mosses, insects and other flora and fauna, as the nutrients once locked in their massive trunks are freed up for other organisms to thrive on for decades to come.

Since the storm, the network of trails through the 301 hectares of ancient trees has been limited, but there is still much to see. On the south side of Alberni Highway, be sure to pay your respects to the largest Douglas fir in the grove, which is an astounding 9 metres in circumference. On the north side of the highway you can explore a large tract of western red cedars near Cameron Lake. Do not forget your phone or camera, as you will most certainly want to document your time spent among such noble giants.

## STRATHCONA PROVINCIAL PARK

# Forbidden Plateau

by Christina Smyth

**The easternmost section of British Columbia's oldest provincial park is a must-do on Vancouver Island regardless of the season**

## What Makes This Hot Spot Hot?

- Unique plant and animal life dominates the landscape, thriving in both the wetlands and the difficult conditions of the alpine meadows.
- The Canada jays in Paradise Meadows are not shy, and visitors will find themselves surrounded by this bird during snack breaks on the trail.
- Views of Vancouver Island's mountains are stunning from Mount Albert Edward, one of the highest peaks on the island.

**Address:** Strathcona Provincial Park, Nordic Dr, Comox-Strathcona, BC
**GPS:** 49.74525; −125.31923
**Tel.:** (844) 435-9453
**Website:** www.env.gov.bc.ca /bcparks/explore /parkpgs/strath

**Open year-round**

Canada jays are abundant in these hemlock forests.

In the heart of Vancouver Island lies the oldest provincial park in British Columbia. Established in 1911, Strathcona Provincial Park boasts over 250,000 hectares of dense forests, alpine peaks, glaciers and waterfalls. It can be difficult to know where to begin! Forbidden Plateau is one of the more easily reachable areas and hosts some of the most spectacular alpine landscapes in the park. Starting in the subalpine hemlock forest near Mount Washington's ski area, visitors can stroll along the Paradise Meadows Trail, where gentle boardwalks move through wetlands abuzz with dragonflies in the warmer months. Many unique and beautiful flowers bloom in the meadows. Violets, monkey flowers and mountain heather thrive in the fields alongside the trails.

Hikers will find themselves surrounded by Canada jays during snack stops and lunch breaks. These friendly and sleek black, grey and white birds are Canada's unofficial national bird. Canada jays may seem to have an insatiable appetite, and to the observer it may seem like they are gathering more than they can eat. The observer may be correct; Canada jays will store food in lichens and under flakes of tree bark to retrieve later in the winter. Like any true Canadian, these birds do not let the snow stop them from going about their business. In March, while Forbidden Plateau is still a winter wonderland, the jays are busy at work on the trunks of coniferous trees building their nests. They gather twigs, bark strips and lichen to form a cup then line it with soft insulating materials, such as animal fur and feathers. The female incubates the eggs and covers the nestlings to keep them warm while the male does most of the work of bringing food to his growing family. Young jays leave their nests in

May, while much of the thick blanket of snow remains on the ground. Researchers are interested in studying the western race of Canada jays found in Paradise Meadows because its appearance and behaviour are notably different from the races that live in the boreal forests and the Rocky Mountains. The Canada jays of Paradise Meadows/ Forbidden Plateau typically live in large social groups of five to 10 birds. More observations will be necessary to answer questions regarding the genetics and behaviour of these birds, but it is possible the western race constitutes a species that is separate from the Canada jays of northern and eastern Canada.

Both Lake Helen Mackenzie and Circlet Lake are fantastic backcountry camping sites. Lake Helen Mackenzie is an easy overnight destination and a relatively level hike from Paradise Meadows. Circlet Lake, which sits in a natural basin and is surrounded by small trees, rests at the foot of a steep incline in the trail along which hikers can continue to Mount Albert Edward, the sixth-highest peak on Vancouver Island. At the peak, hikers are treated to captivating views of the surrounding mountains. Forbidden Plateau is a small but rich slice of paradise that is an excellent gateway to the rest of the park, where there is even more to explore.

↑ A series of trails and boardwalks meanders through meadows and wetlands surrounded by hemlock forests.

↖ Lake Helen Mackenzie features backcountry campsites.

# Golden Ears Provincial Park

by Christina Smyth

**This gigantic park blends outdoor recreation with wilderness preservation**

## What Makes This Hot Spot Hot?

- One of the largest provincial parks in British Columbia, it is part of a much larger green corridor and is home to a diverse population of wildlife.
- This area was the traditional hunting ground for the Coast Salish and Interior Salish First Nations.
- Marshes and forests in valleys and along mountain slopes ring with the songs of the many birds found throughout the park.

**Address:** Golden Ears Pkwy, Maple Ridge, BC
**GPS:** 49.2501; −122.53807
**Tel.:** (604) 466-8325
**Website:** www.env.gov
.bc.ca/bcparks/explore
/parkpgs/golden_ears

**Open year-round**

🚶 🏕 △ 🚴 🏇 ⛷ 🏊 🔭

♿ (Check ahead)

⌕ **Named for its distinctive colouring, the chestnut-backed chickadee is a common sight all year long.**

Just outside the town of Maple Ridge and an easy day trip from Vancouver, Golden Ears is one of the largest provincial parks in British Columbia. Initially part of Garibaldi Provincial Park, north of Squamish, it was separated in 1927. Named for two distinct peaks known as the Golden Ears, the park's 62,540 hectares provide outstanding recreational opportunities in addition to protecting beautiful natural spaces.

Alouette Lake is an excellent camping and swimming spot that attracts locals and visitors from around British Columbia. With numerous beaches and access to many hiking trails, it is easy to see why this lake is so popular. Before becoming a recreational area, the Alouette Valley hosted one of the largest logging operations in the province. A fire in 1931 raged through the valley, and much of the area is now second-growth forest. Nearly 90 years after the fire, it is interesting to hike between the new- and old-growth areas.

After years of logging, the forest in the Alouette Valley

has reclaimed the land for an abundance of flora and fauna. The wildlife is difficult to miss. Pine siskins and chestnut-backed chickadees sing along the trails, and belted kingfishers perch alongside bodies of water. Goats scale rocky cliffs along the alpine mountain, and beavers are known to have dams in the many waterways throughout the park. Northern flying squirrels live in the trees, though they are nocturnal and not easy to see.

The hiking trails are well maintained and offer views of picturesque waterfalls and gorgeous mountains, strolls through both the new- and old-growth forests and access to alpine peaks. The terrain in this park is quite mountainous, so be prepared for some real hiking.

↑ Strolls through lush forests lead to waterfalls and other beautiful sights.

↖ Alouette Lake is a popular destination for day trips and camping.

# E. C. Manning Provincial Park

by Christina Smyth

*Year-round recreational activities encourage visitors to explore the park on foot or by skis or snowshoes*

## What Makes This Hot Spot Hot?

- Every June, a two-day Bird Blitz is hosted in the park, during which birders identify the various birds living in the area.
- The park sits on the northernmost section of the famous Pacific Crest Trail.
- People of all hiking abilities can enjoy the mid-summer bloom of alpine flowers and river otters playing in nearby bodies of fresh water.

**Address:** 7500 Crowsnest Hwy (Hwy 3), Manning Park, BC
**GPS:** 49.08333; −120.83333
**Tel.:** (604) 668-5953
**Website:** www.env.gov .bc.ca/bcparks/explore /parkpgs/ecmanning

Open year-round

&#9855; (Check ahead)

↗ **The view from the Skyline Trail is well worth the effort.**

Lying on the northernmost tip of the Cascade mountain range, E. C. Manning Provincial Park is known as the end of the 4,265-kilometre Pacific Crest Trail, which connects Mexico and Canada. The park's location makes it an ideal spot to get out and stretch your legs when travelling between inland British Columbia and the coast, though it is also a destination for campers and hikers from around the province.

Rhododendron Flats, an easy loop right off the Crowsnest Highway (Highway 3), makes for a spectacular stroll in mid-June. The forest canopy shades areas of beautiful red rhododendrons, which bloom alongside the trail. Although more challenging, the Skyline Trail affords spectacular views of the surrounding mountains. Lightning Lake, a popular campsite, gives visitors access to many hiking trails and the

↑ **Visitors tour Lightning Lake by canoe.**

chance to canoe. All of the trails in the park offer abundant wildlife viewing opportunities, with mammals such as deer, moose, bears, hoary marmots and coyotes roaming the park. On the lake and riverside trails, look for sleek river otters in the water or sunning themselves on the banks.

Strawberry Flats is a marvellous place to stop and birdwatch. The rufous hummingbird and Canada's tiny calliope hummingbird are often spotted in these open meadows. Other popular birding locations include Beaver Pond, where you may see water-loving birds such as sandpipers. Venture into the alpine area to see the white-tailed ptarmigan or grey-crowned rosy-finch. To access this area, follow the Frosty Mountain Trail or hike a section of the Pacific Crest Trail. Alpine flowers are generally in full bloom by mid-summer, so whatever trail you choose to travel, the flowers provide bursts of colour along your journey. Splashes of brilliant purple from the lupines amid red paintbrushes and an array of pinks and yellows are truly a magical sight.

Winter recreation is a large part of Manning Park. Groomed ski trails provide access to views of snow-covered peaks, and winter campsites immerse travellers in the grandeur of an alpine environment blanketed in snow. Whatever the season, prepare to be impressed by the natural beauty of this park.

# Valhalla Provincial Park

by Christina Smyth

**Hikers must prepare to feel an overwhelming sense of awe at the outstanding scenery**

## What Makes This Hot Spot Hot?

- It takes multiple visits to explore this varied park, from its alpine peaks to its lakeside forests.
- High in the alpine environs, mountain goats munch on grass in open fields near rocky slopes, while in the lower-elevation forests, grouse flutter between large trees.
- Pictographs from the Sinixt Nation alongside beautiful lakeshore campsites make canoeing an excellent way to explore the waters.

**Address:** The park is accessible by a number of trailheads and forest service roads as well as by boat from Slocan, Silverton and New Denver, BC
**GPS:** 49.8787; –117.57156
**Tel.:** (800) 689-9025 (Camping reservations)
**Website:** www.env.gov .bc.ca/bcparks/explore /parkpgs/valhalla

**Open year-round**

The Valhalla Range of the Selkirk Mountains is nestled between the Arrow and Slocan Lakes and protects an impressive array of wildlife and habitats. The elevation range enclosed in this protected area means wildlife can move through an entire watershed, from the slightest trickle of snow melting on a mountain to a rushing river or waterfall entering a lake.

The breathtaking scenery of the park is what draws many backcountry campers, hikers and canoeists. Spotting mountain goats as they make their way down steep rocky slopes on a misty morning is truly a magical sight. The park's landscape is characterized by jagged rocky spires, calm alpine lakes surrounded by serene meadows and dense forests of many tree species, including western red cedar and hemlock. Huckleberries grow close to the moss-covered forest floor at lower elevations. Higher up,

blackberries, heather and grasses dominate the landscape between forested areas.

Each environment provides a niche for different animals. Grizzly and black bears, lynx, bobcats, otters and a wide variety of other mammals inhabit various regions of the park. For birders, golden eagles and white-tailed ptarmigans frequent the alpine areas, while grouse, songbirds and waterfowl are abundant throughout the park.

The Gwillim Lakes area is a recommended destination for backcountry hikers and campers. Found at the end of a beautiful trail through amazing alpine forests and along lakes, the Gwillim Lakes are absolutely stunning.

The park is well known by hikers, but canoeing along the lakeshore of Slocan Lake is another a pleasant way to experience the park. There are even marine campsites along the shoreline for those looking to do overnight kayak or canoe trips. Look for pictographs from the Sinixt Nation as you paddle the shoreline.

↑ **The Gwillim Lakes area is a gorgeous destination with a scenic trail.**

↖ **Lucky visitors may spot a lynx from the trails.**

# Kootenay National Park

by Christina Smyth

**Check out the park's unique Paint Pots before taking off on a scenic hike into the forest**

## What Makes This Hot Spot Hot?

- Forest succession following fires in 2003 offers visitors a different visual experience every year.
- The Paint Pots, pools of spring water in ochre beds, are a geological beauty and important to many local Indigenous Peoples.
- Abundant in birds, mountain goats and even grizzly bears, this park is an ever-changing wildlife haven.

**Address:** Banff-Windermere Hwy (Hwy 93), north of Invermere, BC
**GPS:** 50.974685; –115.947277
**Tel.:** (250) 347-9505
**Website:** www.pc.gc.ca /en/pn-np/bc/kootenay/index

**Open year-round**

&#9855; (Check ahead)

Excellent for a wide variety of short excursions, Kootenay National Park has a lot to offer and is relatively easy to access. From glaciers to meadows and mineral baths, this park is an adventure waiting for you. A section of the Burgess Shale, which is an important fossil bed and another nature hot spot, lies in this park. Other main attractions are the Paint Pots, which are cold mineral spring pools sitting in beds of ochre. The shape and colour of the pools make one want to dip a large paintbrush in them! The Niitsitapi, Ktunaxa and Stoney Nations all collected ochre from this area to create paint for various purposes.

The park experienced five lightning wildfires in 2003, and the short Fireweed Loops take hikers on interpretive walks through a burned area. Fireweed and other plants moved in rapidly and are restoring nutrients to the soil. Hiking along these trails is a fantastic opportunity to see a recently burned forest growing and changing. The northern hawk owl, for which burned areas create new habitat, is nesting and living here. Other species that will thrive in the forest as succession continues are grizzly bears and moose. Grizzlies love huckleberries, which generally appear at their best 25 years after a fire.

For something completely different, Marble Canyon Trail leads hikers to a river that cuts through a steep limestone and dolomite gorge, with spectacular mountain views en route. Keep an eye out and you may be lucky enough to spot a bighorn sheep.

With over 200 kilometres of trails, some just off the road and others deep into the backcountry along glaciers and up mountains, this park has something for everybody. And all visitors can agree that an ideal day of fun exploring the park finishes with a soak in the warm waters of Radium Hot Springs.

➤ **Fireweed is a common alpine feature and one of the first plants to regrow in areas affected by forest fires.**

➤ **The northern hawk owl enjoys the habitat created by the park's 2003 fires.**

→ **The Paint Pots sit in ochre beds.**

YOHO NATIONAL PARK

# Burgess Shale

by Christina Smyth

**These rocky slopes protect some of the world's most important fossils**

## What Makes This Hot Spot Hot?

- There are opportunities to learn about the origins of modern plant and animal life while looking at fossils, some of which could be distant ancestors of humans.
- Amazingly detailed fossils preserved from the Cambrian explosion give a glimpse into life over 500 million years ago.
- Visitors can enjoy interpretive tours of two important fossil sites while hiking in the Rocky Mountains.

**Address:** Field, BC
**GPS:** 51.39686; –116.48698
**Tel.:** (800) 343-3006
(Burgess Shale Geoscience Foundation)
**Websites:** www.burgess-shale .bc.ca and www.pc.gc.ca/en /pn-np/bc/yoho/activ/burgess

**Open mid-June through mid-September, when guided hikes are available, conditions permitting**

↑ Scientists were able to create a model of animals such as *Ottoia*, a completely soft-bodied creature, from these well-preserved fossils.

I n Yoho National Park, visitors can see some of the most important fossil beds in the world. The remnants of marine life from 505 million years ago are preserved in the alpine of the Rocky Mountains.

There are two sites to visit in the park, each a rewarding hike with views of the Rockies. The fossilized creatures at these sites give us a glimpse into the Cambrian period, when the first complex animals and ecosystems appeared in the fossil record. Truly representing an explosion of life, some 120 animal fossils found in the Burgess Shale fit into phyla (a classification of living things) that we did not know existed.

Mount Stephen was the first site to be discovered, in 1886, following reports of "stone bugs" being found by railway workers. The tour to the site is a steep but manageable 8-kilometre hike to an abundance of fossils, including many trilobites, which are ancient and extinct arthropods.

In 1909 Charles Walcott, a paleontologist and the leading expert on Cambrian fossils at the time, happened upon a fossil of *Marrella splendens* alongside a trail. With its long head spikes, *M. splendens* is thought to be an ancestor of many modern arthropods, such as crustaceans and arachnids. After following a

path of shale debris up the rocky slope, Walcott discovered what would later be called the Walcott Quarry. The renowned Walcott Quarry tour is a 22-kilometre round trip. The fossils at this quarry are so well preserved that soft body parts are identifiable and can even show who ate who in this ancient ecosystem. A once-bustling ocean saw a sudden landslide of sediment, which created an environment low in oxygen that turned out to be perfect for preserving creatures with mostly or entirely soft bodies, including ancient sponges and worms.

To protect the delicate nature of the sites, visitors require guides. Both the Burgess Shale Geoscience Foundation and Parks Canada offer excellent interpretive tours in which you are able to get up close and learn about many of the fossils. At the quarries, guides talk about the fossils and pass around spectacular examples of each, and then visitors are allowed time to explore the shale on their own. Nearly every overturned rock reveals another fossil.

↑ A charming view of Emerald Lake from the Walcott Quarry.

↓ The hike to the Walcott Quarry includes trails through alpine meadows.

# Wells Gray Provincial Park

by Christina Smyth

**Where viewing iconic waterfalls and spotting bears snatching salmon from the river can be combined into a day trip**

## What Makes This Hot Spot Hot?

- Salmon make an epic journey from the Pacific Ocean to the BC Interior, where bears feed upon them in the river during spawning.
- A number of scenic waterfalls are found in this landscape, which was sculpted by volcanic action and glaciers.
- As an important wildlife corridor, Wells Gray has many opportunities to see wildlife while hiking or canoeing.

**Address:** Clearwater Valley Rd, 10 km north of Clearwater, BC
**GPS:** 51.92815; –120.13195
**Tel.:** (250) 674-3334
**Website:** www.env.gov .bc.ca/bcparks/explore /parkpgs/wells_gry

**Open year-round**

♿ (Check ahead)

Wells Gray Provincial Park protects some of British Columbia's most scenic treasures. Sculpted by glaciers and riddled with volcanic features, this large park in the Interior has expansive stretches of remote wilderness that complement its easily reachable southern section. This combination of accessibility and high-level protection allows the park to thrive, which in turn makes the plants, animals and sights all the more beautiful to behold.

Clearwater Lake, which is surrounded by mountains, is a perfect home base and stunning from both shore and canoe. It was once a large glacier-carved basin that was later dammed by lava and filled with water to create the lake we see today. The outflow of the lake pours over the lava dam, creating Osprey Falls.

Stepping onto one of the park's many trails just off the road, visitors will feel fully immersed in nature, despite being in a popular recreational area. Bears are often sighted alongside creeks hunting for fish. The best time to see them is from August to October, when sockeye

→ **Helmcken Falls is arguably the most majestic waterfall in British Columbia and is easily reachable on foot.**

← **Moose and other wildlife roam the park.**

salmon are spawning and the bears emerge from the forest to feed at the river's edge. One of the most impressive places to view this is Bailey's Chute, where the rivers teem with salmon struggling up the fast-flowing water.

Well-known for its waterfalls, the park hosts the iconic Helmcken Falls, an uninterrupted tower of free-falling water along the Murtle River. Easily one of the most visited sites in the park, this spectacular waterfall is the fourth-highest in Canada and continues to have an amazing impact on the landscape. The rock in the basin, where the water falls, continues to be carved by the falling water.

For the inquisitive mind, there are guided hikes and horseback tours throughout the park, and for the adventurer there are many back-country trails. The alpine meadows and dense forests are home to many animals. Moose utilize Wells Gray as a winter habitat, roaming through snow-covered forests and across fields. The park also hosts many deer and coyotes.

# Mount Robson Provincial Park

by Christina Smyth

**This park is named for a breathtaking peak that towers over meadows, forests and clear alpine streams**

## What Makes This Hot Spot Hot?

- The park protects the headwaters of the Fraser River, which brings life to much of British Columbia.
- Drastic changes in elevation encourage diverse ecosystems, flora and fauna.
- Mount Robson is the tallest of the Canadian Rocky Mountains and has a rich history among the Indigenous Peoples in the area.

**Address:** Off Yellowhead Hwy (Hwy 16), 33 km northeast of Valemont, Fraser-Fort George, BC
**GPS:** 53.03385; –119.23158
**Tel.:** (250) 566-4038
**Website:** www.env.gov .bc.ca/bcparks/explore /parkpgs/mt_robson

**Open year-round**

♿ (Check ahead)

This UNESCO World Heritage Site is home to the highest mountain in the Canadian Rockies, which is also the second-highest in British Columbia. At 2,975 metres, Mount Robson, the park's namesake, is a spectacular rock face. Because of the horizontal strips of coloured rock — limestone, dolomite and quartzite — the people of the Texqakallt Nation refer to the peak as *Yuh-hai-has-kun*, or "the Mountain of the Spiral Road."

Established in 1913 and charged with the important task of protecting the headwaters of the mighty Fraser River, this park is the second-oldest in British Columbia. Downstream, the Fraser River flows through many other nature hot spots before entering the ocean in Vancouver. The river provides life to a large portion of British

Columbia in the form of nutri-ents, a spawning ground, food and water. It is amazing to think that it all begins in this park. Hikers can explore the river's origins on the gentle Fraser River Nature Walk.

There is a wide variety of ecosystems within the park and an abundance of splendid views and wildlife to discover. Every other June the park hosts its Bird Blitz, when birders come together to count the species of birds in the park. There is no shortage, with over 180 recorded species found — including golden eagles in the alpine tundra environment. Elk, bears, Rocky Mountain bighorn sheep and moose live here, among other animals. Bring binoculars if you have them, not just for the birds but also to watch for moun-tain goats on the surrounding cliffs. The plant life here is not inconspicuous either. Lupine, thimbleberry, red cedar, lodge-pole pine and spruce are all found at varying elevations.

Mount Robson Provincial Park deserves a few days, and the Robson Meadows Camp-ground is a fantastic place to make base camp. From there you can explore the wetlands, meadows, forests and alpine environments on the park's many trails.

↑ **Lucky hikers may catch a glimpse of a Rocky Mountain bighorn sheep.**

↖ **Mount Robson towers over the surrounding forest.**

← **Fields of lupine and other wildflowers paint the alpine meadows.**

# Ancient Forest/Chun T'oh Whudujut Provincial Park

by Lyndsay Fraser

*A northern stand of inland old-growth temperate rainforest that is home to 1,000-year-old trees*

## What Makes This Hot Spot Hot?

- Part of the Interior Wet Belt, this is the farthest known inland temperate rainforest in the world.
- Some of the massive western red cedars are thought to be 2,000 years old.
- Around 900 plant species have been identified in the park, including a rare bog orchid.

**Address:** Yellowhead Hwy (Hwy 16) East, 115 km east of Prince George and 103 km west of McBride, BC
**GPS:** 53.763227; −121.218708
**Tel.:** N/A
**Website:** www.env.gov .bc.ca/bcparks/explore /parkpgs/ancient-forest

**Open year-round**

&#9855; (Check ahead)

Situated along the northern limits of the Interior Wet Belt, this stand of trees protected within the boundary of Ancient Forest/ Chun T'oh Whudujut Provincial Park is part of the farthest inland old-growth temperate rainforest known to date, located some 800 kilometres from the ocean. One reason these massive red cedars can thrive so far from the coast is thanks to the heavy snowfall that descends on the forest in the winter. The deep snowpack melts in the spring, restoring water supplies in the ground-water and springs and flood-ing areas of the forest floor.

Aging the trees becomes quite difficult after they have achieved their great size. Although the trees remain alive, giant red cedars often become hollow with age. The heartwood of a tree provides structural support but is com-posed of dead cells, so living tissue can still thrive around a hollow core, leaving in tact the vital conduit between roots and canopy. Some of the trees in the area are upward of 1,000 years old, and some time-worn giants may be closer to 2,000 years old, their age an unsolvable mystery. This truly is an ancient forest.

Trees of this great matur-ity attract a special array of flora and fauna. The park is home to over 200 species of lichen alone! A notable favourite is gold dust lichen, which encrusts the weath-ered and paled cedar trunks and gilds the forest with an extra layer of life. Devil's club inhabits much of the undergrowth. The stems and leaves of this plant are covered with a dense armour of needle-like spines that are extremely irritating if touched. This gives visitors one more reason to stay on the trails, though protecting this rare ecosystem is surely reason enough. During a biological assessment of the park's plant life, bog adder's-mouth

orchids were discovered in the area — the first time this rare species had been documented in the Interior since 1932. The red-listed joe-pye-weed is also found within the boundaries of the park.

This magnificent forest was very close to certain destruction, and it exists today thanks to many passionate individuals working together to ensure the giant trees remained. In 2005 Dave Radies, a graduate student studying old-growth forests of the Interior Cedar-Hemlock Zone, stumbled across this stand and saw telltale forester's red spray-painted on numerous trunks, which meant some of these ancient trees were tagged for removal. After he alerted the public of this special area and its solemn fate, the community rallied together. The following year, the Ancient Forest Trail was built by devoted volunteers, and two years after that the harvesting plans were cancelled. The area was officially designated a provincial park in 2016. The 450-metre boardwalk of the Universal Access Trail ensures that everyone gets to enjoy this unique forest nestled between mountain ranges along the Rocky Mountain Trench.

↑ Devil's club creates dense, and uninviting, undergrowth.

↓ Gold dust lichen covers the trunk of many of the old-growth cedars of this forest.

# Gwaii Haanas

by Christina Smyth

**Protected from sea floor to mountaintop — with mossy rainforests, lively intertidal zones and many of its own subspecies — this park reserve is a treasure**

## What Makes This Hot Spot Hot?

- The lush, ancient rainforest filled with towering cedars inspired Haida activists to lobby to get the southern third of the Haida Gwaii archipelago protected.
- Many distinct and endemic subspecies call these isolated islands home.
- Heritage sites are found throughout the protected area, containing art and architecture that highlights the rich culture of the Haida Nation.

**Address:** Haida Gwaii, BC
**GPS:** 52.46827; –131.5596
**Tel.:** (877) 559-8818
**Website:** www.pc.gc.ca/en /pn-np/bc/gwaiihaanas/index

**Open year-round**

▲ **Humpback whales feed in the chilly waters of the Pacific Northwest.**

Haida Gwaii is a large archipelago separated from British Columbia's west coast. Hecate Strait, which runs up to 140 kilometres across, isolates Haida Gwaii from the Mainland, creating a barrier that has segregated wildlife to the islands. Evolving in isolation, 39 subspecies of plants and animals found nowhere else in the world thrive here. This includes the Haida Gwaii black bear, which has superior jaw strength to its Mainland counterpart — better for crushing hard-shelled critters in the intertidal zone.

Birders, botanizers and marine enthusiasts will all find something to delight them on these islands. Although the number of bird species, approximately 300, is lower than the adjacent Mainland's, there are more unique types to spot, such as the yellow-billed loon and the short-tailed albatross. During the last ice age, British Columbia was blanketed in glaciers; however, back then, parts of Haida Gwaii remained uncovered or were only coated in a thin layer of ice and snow. As a result, some plants here were unaffected by glaciation and quickly repopulated the islands, making this environment particularly special.

Gwaii Haanas National Park Reserve, National Marine Conservation Area Reserve and Haida Heritage Site is the perfect place to experience the wonders of this archipelago. This vast park reserve offers kayaking opportunities to explore the area by water as well as hiking trails, campsites and cultural heritage sites, including those of the Haida Nation that date back some 14,000 years. Visit Hlk'yah GaawGa, where in 2013 a monumental pole was erected to acknowledge the 20th anniversary of the

Gwaii Haanas Agreement and the continued cooperative work between the Council of the Haida Nation and Parks Canada. After resident Haida blocked roads to protest the logging of the archipelago's ancient rainforests, the Gwaii Haanas Agreement was established by the Government of Canada and the Council of the Haida Nation to cooperatively manage and protect the cultural and natural treasures of this area.

Haida Gwaii can be accessed only by boat or seaplane. Your visit to Gwaii Haanas will not be interrupted by the sounds of cars, since there are no roads in the park reserve. To enter, you must reserve a spot, attend a mandatory orientation about travel, safety and the natural and cultural history of the region and then receive a trip permit.

↑ Lush rainforests of towering cedars surround boardwalks and trails.

↖ Poles found on SGang Gwaay mark what was once a community of 300 Haida people.

# Prairie Provinces

## Alberta

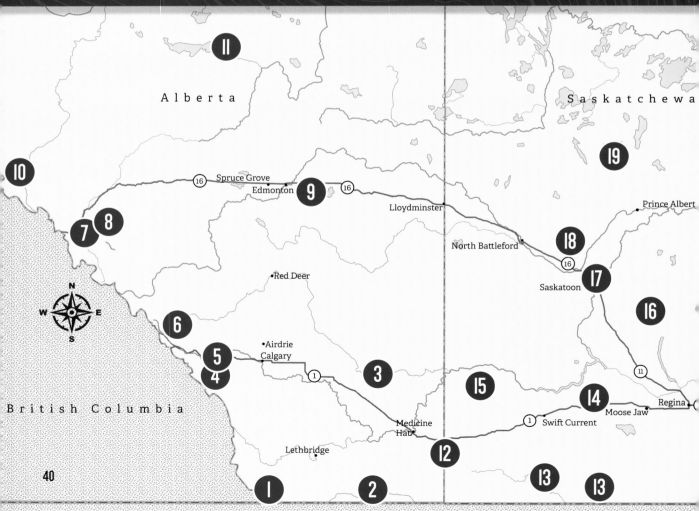

USA

## Saskatchewan

## Manitoba

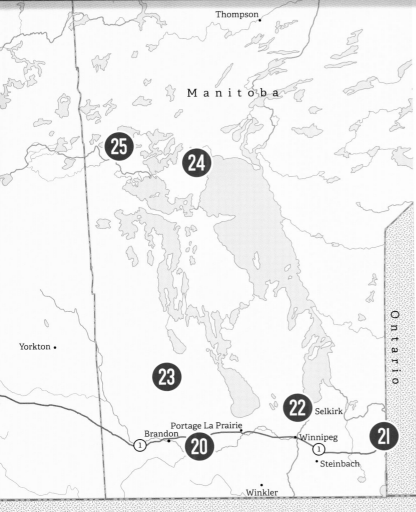

# Waterton Lakes National Park

by Debbie Olsen

*Where the prairies meet the mountains, this small Rocky Mountain park in the southwest corner of Alberta is big on scenery, wildlife and recreation*

## What Makes This Hot Spot Hot?

- Fantastic mountain scenery and a wide array of year-round recreational opportunities are found here.
- The park has excellent conditions for spotting wildlife, and prairies run up the sides of the mountains, making for easy viewing from roadways.
- The Waterton-Glacier International Peace Park was the first park of its kind in the world.

**Address:** 209 Fountain Ave, Waterton Park, AB
**GPS:** 49.0603; –113.9085
**Tel.:** (403) 859-5133
**Website:** www.pc.gc.ca /en/pn-np/ab/waterton

**Open year-round**

&#9855; **(Check ahead)**

The old saying "good things come in small packages" holds true for Waterton Lakes National Park. At 505 square kilometres, Waterton is the smallest of the Canadian Rocky Mountain national parks, but it's also one of the most diverse parks in the national parks system.

Located in a region known as the Crown of the Continent, this park contains beautiful scenery and a vast array of flora and fauna. Over half of Alberta's plant species can be found inside the park, including more than 175 provincially rare plants, such as mountain lady's slipper, pygmy poppy and mountain hollyhock. An annual spring wildflower festival celebrates the diversity of plant life in the park.

There is also an incredible range of wildlife in Waterton Lakes. More than 60 species of mammals, 250 species of birds, 24 species of fish and 10 species of reptiles and amphibians are found here. Large predators include grizzly bears, black bears, wolves, coyotes and cougars. Every autumn the park holds a wildlife festival celebrating its resident animals.

In 1932 Waterton became part of the Waterton-Glacier International Peace Park, a symbol of peace and goodwill between Canada and the United States. You can take a two-hour cruise from the Canadian side of Upper Waterton Lake to the American side (watertoncruise.com). However, if you want to hike on the American side of the lake, you'll need to bring your passport. It's common to see moose on the 4-kilometre Kootenai Lakes hike that departs from Goat Haunt.

There are many wonderful hikes on the Canadian side of Waterton Lakes, including Bear's Hump Trail, Crandell Lake Trail, Rowe Lakes Trail, Carthew-Alderson Trail and the famous Crypt Lake Trail. In 2014 and 2017, *National Geographic* listed the Crypt Lake Trail as one of the "World's 20 Most Thrilling Trails." This unique hike features a 15-minute boat ride across Upper Waterton Lake to the trailhead at Crypt Landing. You'll pass four waterfalls, climb a steel ladder, crawl through an 18-metre tunnel and manoeuvre around a cliff using a steel cable before you arrive at beautiful Crypt Lake.

↑ **The trail to Crypt Lake is one of Canada's premier hikes.**

← **The mountain lady's slipper is a member of the orchid family.**

# Writing-on-Stone Provincial Park/Áisínai'pi National Historic Site

by Debbie Olsen

**_This spectacular valley along the Milk River has long been sacred to Indigenous Peoples and contains many ancient petroglyphs and pictographs_**

## What Makes This Hot Spot Hot?

- This site contains the largest concentration of Indigenous petroglyphs and pictographs on the Great Plains.
- Interpretive programs include storytelling, traditional games, guided tours and wildlife presentations.
- The park features spectacular sandstone rock formations and unique flora and fauna.

**Address:** Range Rd 130A, Aden, AB
**GPS:** 49.0851; –111.6159
**Tel.:** (403) 647-2364
**Website:** www.albertaparks.ca /writing-on-stone

**Open year-round**

A mysterious energy is concealed in the fascinating landscape of Writing-on-Stone Provincial Park. You feel it when you walk among the sandstone hoodoos and gaze at the Sweetgrass Hills that hug the horizon. It's intangible and yet it's not. The peoples of the Blackfoot Confederacy regard land as sacred and ascribe special significance to the hoodoos here. In the past this was a place where young warriors came to fast and pray, some recording their experiences as pictographs (rock paintings) and petroglyphs (rock carvings). Many of these living traditions continue to be practised at Writing-on-Stone/Áisínai'pi, which was designated a UNESCO World Heritage Site in 2019.

Tucked away in the southeast corner of Alberta, near the Montana border, this special spot contains the largest collection of rock art on the

Great Plains of North America, which dates back thousands of years. Historians believe Indigenous Peoples created rock art to depict hunts, battles and important events like vision quests. The peoples of the Blackfoot Confederacy consider the art to be sacred and still return to the area to obtain spiritual guidance.

Rock art is the big attraction here. Even though access to most sites is restricted, park interpreters can take you to places where you can view examples for yourself.

The unusual terrain of the park supports many rare species of plants and animals. Pronghorns roam the grasslands, and raccoons and beaver can sometimes be seen on the river or in ponds. Bobcats, as well as mule and white-tailed deer, can be found in the coulees. It's not uncommon to see bull snakes and prairie rattlesnakes in the park, and it's important to stay on trails and watch where you are walking and sitting.

Visitors can enjoy a wide variety of recreational activities. Paddling or floating the Milk River in a canoe or tube is a marvelous experience, and there is a small sandy beach area along the river's edge that is lovely on a warm summer day. The campground is equipped with RV and tent sites.

↑ **The eroded landscape at Writing-on-Stone Provincial Park is a mesmerizing place to explore.**

← **Ancient petroglyphs are carved in sandstone.**

# Dinosaur Provincial Park

by Debbie Olsen

**_Dinosaurs once roamed the lunar-like landscape of Dinosaur Provincial Park, a UNESCO World Heritage Site that is unlike anywhere else on Earth_**

## What Makes This Hot Spot Hot?

- This UNESCO World Heritage Site contains the highest concentration of late Cretaceous Period fossils in the world.
- Activities include dinosaur digs, bus tours, fossil prospecting, guided hikes and interpretive theatre programs.
- Stunning badlands scenery provides a variety of recreational opportunities.

**Address:** 48 km northeast of Brooks, AB
**GPS:** 50.7594; –111.5190
**Tel.:** (403) 378-4342, ext. 235
**Website:** www.albertaparks.ca/dinosaur

**Open year-round**

 **(Check ahead)**

The landscape of the Canadian Badlands takes you by surprise. One moment you're driving through the flat prairie fields of grass and wheat that are typical of southeastern Alberta. The next, the scenery breaks away to a starkly beautiful landscape of semi-arid steppes, gorges, buttes and oddly misshapen hoodoos. It's an area of exceptional beauty, and the landscape played a part in the decision to make Dinosaur Provincial Park a UNESCO World Heritage Site.

It's hard to imagine this place as a subtropical paradise, but millions of years ago, this park was filled with palm trees and ferns. Dinosaurs roamed on the edge of a great inland sea. There were so many dinosaurs that this spot contains the world's highest concentration of late Cretaceous period fossils.

The outstanding number and variety of high-quality fossil specimens inside the park is the second major consideration for its UNESCO designation. Every known group of Cretaceous dinosaurs is found here. More than 300 specimens have been extracted from the Oldman Formation in the park, including more than 150 complete skeletons, which now reside in more than 30 major museums. Many fossils still lie waiting to be uncovered, and the opportunities for paleontological discovery are great.

This park has incredible interpretive programs that teach visitors about dinosaurs, show them how to identify fossils and even provide opportunities to excavate fossils with real scientists. There are also guided badlands hikes and interpretive theatre programs.

The final reason for the park's UNESCO designation: it protects 26 kilometres of riparian habitat along the banks of the Red Deer River. Hike the Cottonwood Flats Trail, and enjoy a leisurely walk along the riverside under a canopy of cottonwood trees while looking for wildlife along the way.

Dinosaur Provincial Park provides diverse habitats for a wide variety of mammals, reptiles, amphibians and birds.

You might see pronghorn antelope, mule deer, bobo-links, lark buntings, Brewer's sparrows, yellow-breasted chats and more. Over 165 species of birds have been seen here, with 64 species nesting regularly. There is a significant number of breeding birds of prey, including golden eagles, ferruginous hawks, prairie falcons, merlins, northern harriers and kestrels.

This park has wonderful trails to explore and excellent campground facilities for tents and RVs. Alberta Parks also has comfort camping facilities in the form of semi-permanent canvas-walled tents with wood floors, real beds and handmade furnishings.

↑ **Badlands and hoodoos form a dramatic landscape.**

→ **Visitors young and old can find fossils in Dinosaur Provincial Park.**

# Peter Lougheed and Spray Valley Provincial Parks

by Debbie Olsen

*These two parks protect 76,740 hectares of land in the front ranges of the Rockies, a scenic area of high ecological importance*

## What Makes This Hot Spot Hot?

- Recreational opportunities abound in the Upper Kananaskis, Smith-Dorrien and Spray Valleys.
- This breathtaking scenery is home to a wide array of plant and animal species.
- The park features year-round, barrier-free wilderness lodging and trails.

**Address:** Peter Lougheed Discovery Centre, Kananaskis Lakes Trail, Kananaskis, AB
**GPS:** PLPP: 50.68609; –115.11354 SVPP: 50.8891, –115.2951
**Tel.:** (403) 678-0760
**Websites:** www.albertaparks .ca/peter-lougheed and www.albertaparks.ca /spray-valley

**Open year-round**

♿ **(Check ahead)**

These two parks are both part of Kananaskis Country, an area of park land about 90 kilometres west of Calgary. There are 10 provincial parks in all and one ecological reserve in Kananaskis Country. The area gets its name from the river that passes through it. In 1858 John Palliser, an Irish-born geographer and explorer, named the Kananaskis River after a Cree acquaintance. He probably never anticipated that the entire region would someday be known by that name.

The parks in Kananaskis Country are incredibly popular with locals and visitors alike. Peter Lougheed and Spray Valley Provincial Parks are located near the Great Divide, in the front ranges of the Rocky Mountains, and the scenery is glorious.

A wide array of wildlife species can be found here. You might see mule deer, white-tailed deer, elk, moose,

bighorn sheep, mountain goats, grizzly and black bears, cougars, wolves, wolverines, lynx and coyotes as well as smaller mammals typical of alpine and subalpine habitats. There's also a wide array of flora to be discovered in the montane, alpine and sub-alpine terrains of these parks. The forests of Peter Lougheed Provincial Park are mostly lodgepole pine, while the forests in Spray Valley Provincial Park are dominated by spruce and fir trees. The differences in the forests' compositions are attributed to the frequency of wildfires.

Too often, wilderness areas are inaccessible to people with disabilities, but that is not the case here. The William Watson Lodge in Peter Lougheed Provincial Park provides year-round accessible wilderness lodging for seniors and people with disabilities, by reserva-tion only. The facility allows people of all abilities and ages to enjoy the park. There are more than 20 kilometres of accessible trails near the lodge as well as cabins, RV sites and picnic areas.

These parks can be very busy, thanks to all the wonder-ful trails, scenery and recrea-tional opportunities they provide. Visitors should make reservations at campgrounds or lodges in advance, espe-cially for the summer months.

↑ **Wildflowers bloom in Spray Valley Provincial Park.**

← **Sunlight filtering through the dense trees lends beauty and drama to this forest scene.**

# Bow Valley Provincial Park

by Leigh McAdam

**This natural gem is located at the intersection of three ecosystems — grasslands, mountains and boreal forest**

## What Makes This Hot Spot Hot?

- The park has excellent wildlife-viewing opportunities, including birdwatching.
- Bow Valley is located at the intersection of three unique ecosystems.
- There are plenty of summer activities, including hiking, biking and canoeing.

**Address:** Hwy 1X (Trans-Canada Hwy), about 85 km west of Calgary, AB
**GPS:** 51.0510; −115.0727
**Tel.:** (403) 673-3663; (403) 678-0760 (Barrier Lake)
**Website:** www.albertaparks .ca/bow-valley-pp

**Open year-round; Bow Valley Campground is closed to vehicles from Thanksgiving to late April**

&#9855; **(Check ahead)**

Located less than an hour's drive west of Calgary, Bow Valley Provincial Park is home to a diverse landscape that includes the front range of the Canadian Rockies, grasslands, boreal forests and a section along the glacier-fed Bow River. You'll find lots to do, from canoeing and hiking to cycling, horseback riding and nature viewing.

The park is irregularly shaped and divided in the north by the Trans-Canada Highway. There are a couple of kayak launches and picnic areas along Highway 40, but the bulk of the park is explored via two main entry points: off the Trans-Canada Highway at Highway 1X and at the entrance to Barrier Dam off Highway 40 (Kananaskis Trail).

## Northern Entry Point off Highway IX

This part of the park presents a rich ecosystem and is home to a diverse array of birds, from the diminutive rufous hummingbird to the bald eagle. If you snag a campsite along the beautiful Bow River, you can enjoy watching ducks and geese that fly through the area from the front door of your tent. Bring a bike and cycle the roads, keeping a close eye out for wildlife like wolves, mule deer, elk, moose and bears.

You can also hike one of the seven trails. All are easy, most offer outstanding mountain views and, despite their short distances, they cover many diverse ecosystems. In summer the most popular trail is the 1.6-kilometre Many Springs Trail, which loops through a spring-fed wetland, where the temperature remains constant year-round. Deer and elk are drawn to the minerals in the spring. In June the trail is dotted with bright yellow lady's slipper. The 1.5-kilometre Montane Trail is also worth an hour. It showcases the challenging transition zone where the foothills meet the mountains.

## Barrier Dam and Barrier Lake

Turquoise-coloured Barrier Lake is a beautiful place to stop and explore. Birding is good along the lake, the mountain vistas enchant and there are plenty of early-season wildflowers. You can enjoy the lake from one of several picnic spots along the east shore, but for a more intimate experience go paddling, boating or fishing. You can also explore the west side of the lake from a trail starting at the dam. It's accessible to horseback riders, cyclists and hikers.

↑ **This stunning view of turquoise-coloured Barrier Lake is the reward for mountain hikers.**

# Banff National Park

by Debbie Olsen

*Canada's first national park is home to dramatic mountain peaks, glistening lakes, hot springs, a vast array of wildlife and a picture-perfect mountain town*

## What Makes This Hot Spot Hot?

- Banff is the flagship of Canada's national parks system and part of a UNESCO World Heritage Site.
- There are wonderful hiking opportunities on more than 1,600 kilometres of maintained trails.
- The park's vast array of flora and fauna includes bears, elk, moose, deer, wolves, foxes, coyotes and bighorn sheep.

**Address:** 224 Banff Ave, Banff, AB
**GPS:** 51.17794; –115.57041
**Tel.:** (403) 762-1550
**Website:** www.pc.gc.ca/en /pn-np/ab/banff/index

**Open year-round; visitor centre hours vary by season**

&#9855; **(Check ahead)**

The discovery of natural hot springs in 1883 prompted the Canadian government to create Canada's first national park. Incredible scenery and adventures are found within its 6,641 square kilometres.

## Banff Townsite Area

There's much to see and do in and around the mountain town of Banff. If you don't have a vehicle, you can use the Roam public transit system to get to many of the key sites inside town as well as travel to Canmore and Lake Louise. Here are a few of the must-see stops in and around Banff:

***Bow Falls*** Located near the Banff Springs Hotel, these falls were featured in the 1953 Marilyn Monroe film *River of No Return*.

***Cave and Basin National Historic Site*** A visit to this site will tell you more about the culture and history of this region

and how Canada's national parks system was born.

**Banff Gondola** Take this gondola to the top of Sulphur Mountain for an incredible view of the Bow Valley.

**Banff Upper Hot Springs** Soak in the naturally heated hot pools that have been a highlight of Banff for over a century.

**Lake Minnewanka** The largest lake in the park is a 15-minute drive from the Banff town centre. You can enjoy a one-hour interpretive cruise or just drive the Lake Minnewanka Loop. It's one of the best places to spot wildlife — especially at dusk.

**Vermillion Lakes** Three beautiful lakes and magnificent Mount Rundle are a 5-minute drive from the centre of Banff.

## Johnston Canyon

This deep canyon is one of the most stunning geological features of Banff National Park and one of the most popular day hikes. It's best to go early to avoid crowds. A paved hiking trail and metal catwalk make this canyon accessible. It's an easy 1.2-kilometre walk to the Lower Falls and a moderate 2.4-kilometre climb to the 30-metre-high Upper Falls.

To reach the Ink Pots, continue 3 kilometres further on from the Upper Falls. The moderate climb out of the

↑ Well-constructed bridges and trails make Johnston Canyon a pleasurable family hiking destination.

← The river plummets 9.1 metres at Bow Falls.

↑ **Mind-blowing wildflower displays can be found above Sunshine Meadows at Healey Pass.**

↗ **The Larch Valley is one of Banff's most popular fall hikes — and for good reason, as this golden landscape shows.**

canyon takes about an hour and leads to several pools of emerald-coloured mineral springs that bubble to the surface at a constant temperature of about 4°C — even in winter.

Watch for wildlife in the canyon and on the drive leading to it. It's possible to see owls, osprey, eagles, elk, deer, bighorn sheep, black bears and grizzly bears while driving along the parkway.

## Lake Louise and Moraine Lake

Surrounded by rugged peaks, the awe-inspiring beauty of these two sparkling lakes is a highlight of Banff National Park. The two lakes attract famously large crowds — especially during the peak summer

months, but a little crowd dodging is worth it to take in the spectacular scenery.

Parks Canada operates free shuttles from Banff townsite to Lake Louise during the peak summer months and to Moraine Lake during September, when larch hiking is popular. You can rent a canoe and enjoy a peaceful paddle on either lake or hike one of the many area trails.

From Lake Louise, you can hike to Lake Agnes Tea House or the Plain of Six Glaciers Tea House. If you hike to both tea houses in a single day, you will have conquered the "Tea House Challenge."

The Larch Valley is accessed from Moraine Lake and is a spectacular hike in September, when the larch trees turn yellow and their needles begin to drop. There are many trails, and it's possible to find solitude even in the most popular spot in Canada's first national park.

## Sunshine Meadows

These high alpine meadows are one of the prettiest day hikes in the Canadian Rockies. The meadows are readily accessible to even novice hikers via a gondola and chairlift. Located on the continental divide, the trails here cover terrain in both Alberta and British Columbia. You can take a short walk on the trails near the chairlift or

hike to Rock Isle Lake or Healy Pass. The scenery is stunning, particularly from mid-July to late August, when wildflowers carpet the meadows. Keep an eye out for bighorn sheep, mountain goats and grizzly bears.

## Bow Summit and Peyto Lake Lookout

A view of the stunning turquoise-blue Peyto Lake is the highlight of a stop along the highest drivable pass in Banff National Park. It's a short hike from the parking lot to Peyto Lake Lookout, where you can see beautiful Peyto Lake, Peyto Glacier and the vast Mistaya Valley. Continue following the trail and you'll arrive at more views of Peyto and the less-travelled Bow Lake Lookout, which offers views of the Icefields Parkway, Bow Glacier and Bow Lake.

Lakes in the Canadian Rockies get their brilliant blue colour from glacial rock flour. Glacial erosion causes silt particles to flow into the lake water, and these suspended particles reflect light, giving the lakes their stunning turquoise colour.

# Jasper National Park

by Debbie Olsen

*Ancient glaciers, rugged mountain peaks, crystal clear lakes and abundant wildlife can be found in Canada's largest Rocky Mountain park*

## What Makes This Hot Spot Hot?

- The incredible mountain scenery includes the largest and most accessible icefield in the Rocky Mountains.
- The park, which is excellent for wildlife watching, provides habitat for 53 species of mammals, including grizzly and black bears.
- The area is home to five National Historic Sites.

**Address:** 500 Connaught Dr, Jasper, AB
**GPS:** 52.87727; –118.0807
**Tel.:** (780) 852-6236
**Website:** www.pc.gc.ca/en /pn-np/ab/jasper/index

**Open year-round**

&#9855; (Check ahead)

Jasper is the largest and wildest of Canada's Rocky Mountain parks, and there is much to see and do within its 10,878 square kilometres.

## Maligne Valley

Carved by ancient glaciers, the Maligne Valley contains some of the most spectacular scenery in the Canadian Rockies and is home to a wide variety of plants and animals. Maligne Lake Road is one of the best places in the park for viewing wildlife.

Maligne Lake is the largest natural lake in the Canadian Rockies, and Spirit Island is one of Jasper's iconic features. You can rent canoes at the lake and enjoy a peaceful paddle, or Brewster Travel Canada offers a 90-minute boat cruise to Spirit Island.

Maligne Canyon is another highlight. Hikers can follow a 4.4-kilometre return trail that winds along the canyon edge to spectacular viewpoints and over six bridges. The canyon is impressive in every season. In the winter, guided ice walks are offered by a handful of tour companies.

There are several wonderful hikes that depart from or

traverse the Maligne Valley, including the Opal Hills Loop, the Bald Hills Trail and the iconic Skyline Trail, one of the premier backpacking trails in the Canadian Rockies.

## Mount Edith Cavell and Area

Mount Edith Cavell is a majestic 3,300-metre peak that is an icon in Jasper National Park and one of the most recognizable peaks in the Canadian Rockies. Area trails offer views of the Angel Glacier and meadows filled with summer wildflowers.

The Path of the Glacier Trail is a short 1.6-kilometre return paved trail that goes from the parking area toward the north face of the mountain. The trail ends with a viewpoint overlooking Cavell Pond and the layered ice of Cavell Glacier.

Cavell Meadows Trail is a moderately difficult 7-kilometre return hike that offers wonderful views of the Angel Glacier and alpine meadows. In mid-July, you'll find meadows filled with colourful wildflowers. Look for Indian paintbrush, forget-me-nots and cinquefoil, to name a few.

## Pyramid Lake and Patricia Lake

At the foot of Pyramid Mountain, Pyramid Lake and nearby Patricia Lake are two of the prettiest recreational areas

↑ **Mount Edith Cavell towers over a turquoise glacial lake formed from the Angel Glacier.**

← **Spirit Island is one of the most photographed spots in the Maligne Valley.**

↑ **Don't miss the walk out to and around Pyramid Island.**

↓ **Woodland caribou are a special sight in the Tonquin Valley.**

public area with bench seating for up to 50 people, which can be rented for inexpensive outdoor weddings with million-dollar views.

Patricia Lake is the quieter of the two lakes, but as they say, still waters run deep. The lake is popular with scuba divers, since a top-secret World War II prototype vessel lies at the bottom of it.

## Tonquin Valley

Situated at the continental divide, the Tonquin Valley is a lovely spot in the backcountry of Jasper National Park. Beautiful Amethyst Lake and the rugged Rampart Mountains are scenic highlights. Visitors to this area may get the chance to see two rare species: the woodland caribou and the whitebark pine. The valley is home to a small herd of woodland caribou, a species at risk in Jasper National Park. The endangered whitebark pine only grows at high elevations and can be found along the first few kilometres of the Astoria Trail.

## Columbia Icefield

This massive icefield is made up of about 30 glaciers and covers an area around 325 square kilometres. It is surrounded by stunning mountain peaks and is the largest and most accessible icefield in

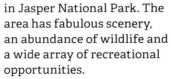

in Jasper National Park. The area has fabulous scenery, an abundance of wildlife and a wide array of recreational opportunities.

In summer, you can rent canoes, kayaks, row boats, paddleboats, mountain bikes and electric cruiser bikes at Pyramid Lake Lodge. In winter, they offer skate, snowshoe and fat bike (also called snow bike) rentals as well as horse-drawn sleigh rides. An area of the lake is kept clear for skating in winter, and if you bring cross-country skis, you can ski on the frozen lake or the groomed trails just off Pyramid Road.

Be sure to take a walk out to Pyramid Island. It's a short jaunt from the roadway and has a lovely picnic area and a

the Rocky Mountains — reachable by car via the Icefields Parkway.

One of the glaciers of the Columbia Icefield, the Athabasca Glacier, is visible from the main roadway, and a short hike takes you to the glacier's toe. At the Columbia Icefield Glacier Discovery Centre, you can see a photo gallery that shows how much the Athabasca Glacier has receded over time. In the last 125 years, it has receded more than 1.5 kilometres and lost over half of its volume. You can also book tours to explore the glacier's surface on an Athabasca Glacier Ice Explorer bus.

There are two wonderful hikes near the Columbia Icefield Glacier Discovery Centre. The Forefield Trail is the easiest hike. It is 3.4-kilometre return journey and follows the barren area left by the retreating glacier. If you're up for a bigger challenge, try hiking Wilcox Pass. The trail is steep, but you get amazing views of the glacier, and you're almost certain to see bighorn sheep. It takes about an hour to hike to the first viewpoint and 2 to 3 hours to hike the entire 8-kilometre return trail.

↑ **The sprawling Columbia Icefield snakes through the Rocky Mountains.**

# Whitehorse Wildland Provincial Park

by Leigh McAdam

**A little-known park that's wild, beautiful and rich in plant species and wildlife**

## What Makes This Hot Spot Hot?

- This is one of the few places in Alberta where you can drive to an alpine meadow.
- Cadomin Cave provides important habitat for bats; it's one of only four spots in Alberta where bats can overwinter.
- The park contains over 277 plant species, including many rare specimens.

**Address:** Range Rd 235A, 6 km south of Cadomin, AB
**GPS:** 52.98443; –117.34986
**Tel.:** (780) 865-8395; (780) 865-2154 (camping reservations)
**Website:** www.albertaparks .ca/whitehorse

**Whitehorse Creek Provincial Recreation Area is open year-round; Cardinal Divide is open from mid-June until Thanksgiving, depending on weather**

If you love truly wild places, head to Whitehorse Wildland Provincial Park, located about an hour's drive south of Hinton. The park shares its western border with Jasper National Park. Visitors can explore the park on foot from the Cardinal Divide Viewpoint parking lot or via a backcountry trail that begins at the Whitehorse Creek Provincial Recreation Area. The trail to Cadomin Cave (Alberta's largest bat hibernation cave) has been temporarily closed at the time of printing to reduce the risk of white-nose syndrome, a fungal disease that kills cave-roosting bats.

## The Cardinal Divide

If you head for the Cardinal Divide, a high clearance vehicle is recommended. The drive up the dirt road passes an active coal mine with massive trucks at work on their own dedicated road. Once you get past the mine, you'll be struck by the beauty of the surrounding wilderness. The Cardinal Divide sits at an elevation of 1,981 metres on the division of two major river systems — the McLeod River and the Cardinal River. It's prime habitat for a variety of animals, including elk, moose, mule deer, bighorn sheep, black bears, wolves, cougars, marmots and pikas.

The area around the Cardinal Divide can only be explored on foot, and camping is not permitted. Extensive alpine meadows, renowned for their summer wildflowers and subalpine slopes, will beckon the hiker. Stay on the unmarked trails to protect the very fragile soil and plants. Another hiking option is to follow the dirt track from the parking lot east up the ridge for gorgeous views of the upper foothills.

## Whitehorse Creek Provincial Recreation Area

It's also possible to hike, backpack or horseback ride into the park from the Whitehorse Creek Provincial Recreation Area. To find it, look for a turnoff marked "camping" on the road up to the Cardinal Divide, not far from Cadomin. There are campsites by the trailhead that can also accommodate horses. If you choose to camp in the winter, note that roads into the area are not maintained, and you should be very familiar with backcountry camping in the winter before venturing in.

The Lower Whitehorse Trail takes you through prime grizzly country, so be bear aware. There are several options for multi-day backpacking trips, including one over Fiddle Pass and into Jasper National Park. As you hike or ride, look for some of the 277 different plant species that live in the park, including 37 that are rare. One, a moss named *Bryum porsildii*, is found only at a few other locations in the world. At the lower elevations you may also spot harlequin ducks and some of the 128 bird species in the park.

⬆ **Visitors can drive right up to this high-alpine meadow.**

# Beaver Hills Biosphere

by Debbie Olsen

*This UNESCO-designated biosphere reserve encompasses 1,572 square kilometres of predominantly natural landscape east of Edmonton*

## What Makes This Hot Spot Hot?

- There are 35 lakes and almost 700 campsites within the biosphere.
- The Beaver Hills Biosphere is situated in a distinct geographical region that includes boreal forests and wetlands.
- The area supports both boreal forest and parkland animals, including up to 48 mammal, 152 bird and 8 amphibian and reptile species.

**Address:** 54401 Range Rd 203, Fort Saskatchewan, AB (Elk Island National Park)
**GPS:** 53.57875; –112.83821 (Elk Island National Park)
**Tel.:** (780) 922-5790 (Elk Island National Park); (780) 672-7274 (Miquelon Lake Provincial Park)
**Website:** www.albertaparks.ca and www.ealt.ca

**Open year-round**

&#9855; **(Check ahead; Elk Island and Miquelon Lake have some accessible services)**

The Beaver Hills Biosphere is a distinct geographical region of forests, wetlands, small lakes and streams. There are several protected areas to experience in the biosphere.

## Elk Island National Park

This national park is Canada's only entirely fenced national park and one of its smallest, at 194 square kilometres. It is home to the densest population of hoofed mammals in Canada, an important refuge for elk and one of the few places you can see plains and wood bison roaming freely. Moose, mule deer and white-tailed deer are also commonly spotted.

The park is home to more than 250 bird species. Notable bird species include trumpeter swans, red-necked grebes, double-crested cormorants, red-tailed hawks, American bitterns, American white pelicans and great blue herons. The park is located approximately 48 kilometres east of Edmonton off Highway 16.

## Ministik Lake Game Bird Sanctuary

When it was established in 1911, the Ministik Lake Game Bird Sanctuary was Alberta's first provincial bird sanctuary. American white pelicans, blue herons, bald eagles, horned grebes, ducks and a wide variety of waterfowl and songbirds are commonly seen in the 7,349-hectare site. Moose, deer, coyotes, wolves and small mammals might also be spotted. Ministik can be accessed 24 kilometres southeast of Edmonton, off Township Road 510.

## Cooking Lake-Blackfoot Provincial Recreational Area

There are more than 170 kilometres of trails in this 97-square-kilometre all-season recreation area. It is the site of the annual Canadian Birkebeiner Ski Festival, the largest classic-style cross-country ski festival in Canada. It's also a great destination for hiking, mountain biking, horseback riding and snowshoeing. In summer, look for nesting pairs

of trumpeter swans and other waterfowl. You might also see coyotes, deer, elk, foxes, moose and lynx. You can access the provincial recreational area off of Range Road 210, about 8 kilometres south of Highway 16.

## Miquelon Lake Provincial Park

Explore this 1,299-hectare park on one of the many mountain biking trails or its accessible paved shoreline path. At the Miquelon Visitor Centre, you can rent a family discovery pack for a small fee and learn about the flora and fauna. The park is located off of Highway 623 (Rollyview Road).

## Golden Ranches Conservation Site

On the east shore of Cooking Lake, this 567-hectare site provides a home for many bird species and serves as a staging area for migratory birds. A mixture of aspen forest and open grassland provides habitat for white-tailed and mule deer, moose, grouse, porcupines and a variety of small mammals. The site is 45 kilometres east of Edmonton, off Township Road 515. A detailed map can be found on the Edmonton and Area Land Trust Society website.

## Beaver Hills Dark Sky Preserve

This 300-square-kilometre dark sky preserve is entirely within the Beaverhills Biosphere and encompasses Elk Island National Park, Miquelon Lake Provincial Park and Cooking Lake-Blackfoot Provincial Recreation Area. An annual Star Party is held each September.

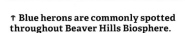

↑ Blue herons are commonly spotted throughout Beaver Hills Biosphere.

↖ A visitor observes bison in Elk Island National Park.

↓ Families can rent a discovery pack for a day of nature-oriented adventure at Miquelon Lake Provincial Park.

# Willmore Wilderness Park and Sulphur Gates

by Leigh McAdam

**_Explore a vast wilderness park known for its spectacular mountain scenery and plentiful wildlife_**

## What Makes This Hot Spot Hot?

- Sulphur Gates offers superlative views of the Sulphur River Canyon, where it meets the Smoky River.
- At 4,597 square kilometres, Willmore Wilderness Park is the largest wilderness area in Alberta.
- There's a high density of wildlife in Willmore Wilderness Park.

**Address:** Sulphur Gates Rd, near Grand Cache, AB
**GPS:**
Sulphur Gates: 53.8712; –119.1875
Willmore: 53.6855; –119.0745
**Tel.:** (780) 827-7393;
(780) 865-8395
**Websites:** www.albertaparks .ca/sulphur-gates and www.albertaparks.ca/willmore

**Open year-round; roads are not maintained in winter**

Sulphur Gates Provincial Recreation Area and Willmore Wilderness Park meet just west of Grande Cache. Sulphur Gates can easily be visited and enjoyed over an hour or two, but Willmore Wilderness, the largest wilderness area in Alberta, needs more time to be fully appreciated.

The Sulphur Gates area offers limited recreational opportunities. People visit to be wowed by the spectacular views of the confluence of the Sulphur and Smoky Rivers and the Sulphur River Canyon. You can enjoy the views via a short trail from the parking lot.

Sulphur Gates is one of three access points to Willmore Wilderness Park and acts as a staging area for both backpackers and equestrians. Day hikers can enjoy a 3-kilometre trail to Eaton Falls in the Willmore Wilderness. The falls themselves are quite lovely, and along the way there's a marvelous viewpoint.

Despite its massive size, Willmore Wilderness Park is virtually unknown. But if you're well-equipped for backcountry adventures, either on foot or on horse, you can explore its 750 kilometres of trails.

The Willmore area is known for broad, grass-covered valleys, green subalpine and alpine ridges, alpine meadows, mountain peaks and glaciers on some of the high mountains. Six rivers criss-cross the park, with all but the Smoky River originating in the park. The scenery is spectacular — rugged mountains, lots of wildflowers, waterfalls, rapids and a sense of space in a huge expanse of wilderness.

Wildlife in the park includes mountain caribou, grizzly and black bears, cougars, wolves, moose, elk, mountain goats and bighorn sheep. Birds include boreal and mountain species along with harlequin ducks in wetland areas.

Rock Lake Provincial Park is the access point that's most

↑Viewing platforms around Sulphur Gates allow visitors to experience breathtaking views of Willmore Wilderness Park.

used to visit Willmore. It's a 90-minute drive from Hinton via Highway 40 followed by a 30-kilometre drive on a dirt road. The third option is via Big Berland Recreation Area off Highway 40.

Most people visit the park on horseback via original pack trails that have deep ruts and gouges — not the best trails for hiking. It's recommended that hikers allow a minimum of four days to experience the park. Your best bet is to set up a base camp and do day hikes up to the ridge tops to enjoy the views for which the park is famous. By sticking to the main valley trails, hikers will miss much of the park's beauty.

Adventurous types eager to explore a little-visited part of Alberta will find plenty to love on a trip to Willmore Wilderness Park.

→ The Sulphur River is framed on both sides by dramatically steep valley walls.

# Lesser Slave Lake Provincial Park

by Debbie Olsen

**The third-largest lake in Alberta has beautiful beaches and is a designated Important Bird Area**

## What Makes This Hot Spot Hot?

- Lesser Slave Lake is rimmed with some of the finest beaches in Alberta.
- This area is a fine example of the boreal forest region.
- The Boreal Centre for Bird Conservation is a great place to observe and learn about migratory birds.

**Address:** Boreal Centre for Bird Conservation, Hwy 88, 19 km north of Slave Lake, AB
**GPS:** 55.41234; –114.80468
**Tel.:** (780) 849-8240; Park Info Line (mid-May to early September): (780) 849-2111; Off-season: (780) 849-7100
**Websites:** www.albertaparks .ca/lesser-slave-lake-pp and www.borealbirdcentre.ca

**Open year-round**

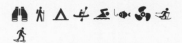

&#9855; **(Limited, check ahead)**

When a strong wind blows waves across Alberta's third-largest lake, you can almost believe you're at the edge of the ocean as you gaze out from the sandy shoreline. At nearly 1,200 square kilometres, Lesser Slave Lake is rimmed by some of the finest beaches in the entire province and is a wonderful place to visit on a warm summer day. It's also a great place to see sand dunes, hike and watch wildlife.

Lesser Slave Lake is a prime fishing lake, and the forests that surround it teem with wildlife. For these reasons, the region was well-known to the Beaver and Woodland Cree, two Indigenous Peoples who lived and hunted in the region. David Thompson was the first European to reach Lesser Slave Lake, arriving in 1799. He commented on the abundance of moose, bison and waterfowl, and he made detailed survey observations to map the area. Fur-trading posts were eventually built on the shores of the lake by the North West and Hudson's Bay Companies, and Lesser Slave Lake became one of the most productive fur-bearing regions in Canada.

A unique microclimate and the rich habitat of the boreal forest make this area a haven for nesting and migratory birds — especially songbirds. The area has been designated an Important Bird Area. Experts have dubbed the boreal forest region "North America's bird nursery" because so many bird species nest and raise their young in and around the Lesser Slave Lake district.

Many birds pass through this region during their spring and fall migrations, and it's estimated that up to 20 per cent of the western population of tundra swans stops to feed on the lake. Flocks of up to 3,500 swans have been documented in the spring and fall. Reeds around the lake provide nesting habitat for a globally

important western grebe population. The area also has an incredible concentration and diversity of migrant songbirds, including the yellow warbler, bay-breasted warbler and red-eyed vireo, to name a few. Visitors with a particular interest in songbirds should hike the Songbird Trail or attend the Songbird Festival, held in the park each spring.

↑ The sandy and rocky shores of Lesser Slave Lake are great for a scenic stroll.

→ Outdoor activities are offered year-round, like cross-country skiing in the winter.

# Cypress Hills Interprovincial Park

by Debbie Olsen

*Canada's first interprovincial park is a haven for geologists, naturalists and outdoor enthusiasts alike*

## What Makes This Hot Spot Hot?

- The Cypress Hills plateau is the highest point between the Rockies and Labrador.
- Cypress Hills is home to diverse flora and fauna.
- This park offers a wide variety of all-season recreational opportunities.

**Addresses:** Alberta: 8304 Hwy 41, Cypress County, AB
West Block: Hwy 271, about 55 km south of Maple Creek, SK
Centre Block: Ben Nevis Dr., Maple Creek, SK
**GPS:** Alberta: 49.66032; –110.28691
West Block: 49.57552; –109.87378
Centre Block: 49.66037; –109.50174
**Tel.:** Alberta: (403) 893-3833
Saskatchewan: (306) 662-5411
**Website:** www.cypresshills.com

**Alberta and Centre Block are open year-round; West Block is open May long weekend to Labour Day**

♿ (Check ahead)

The Cypress Hills have been called "an island of forest in a sea of grassland." Millions of years ago, during the last ice age, the top 100 metres of the plateau were quite literally an island in a sea of ice. Rising high above the surrounding prairie, the unusual geology and high elevation give this area a unique climate that provides for a wide variety of ecosystems with diverse plant and animal life. At least 18 species of orchid grow here — more than anywhere else on the Prairies.

It's common to see elk, mule deer, white-tailed deer, bison, pine martens and cougars in the park. It's also one of the best birdwatching locations in Canada, with more than 220 recorded species. The interprovincial park straddles an area on the southern border of Saskatchewan and Alberta. It can be divided into three main areas: Alberta, West Block and Centre Block.

## Alberta

Less than an hour's drive southeast of Medicine Hat, you'll find the major facilities for the Alberta side of Cypress Hills Interprovincial Park along the south shore of Elkwater Lake. There are 11 campgrounds throughout the park with services for tents, RVs and trailers, as well as one equestrian campground with horse corrals and hitching rails. Alberta Parks also offers furnished comfort camping cabins and huts equipped with soft beds and kitchen facilities. At the Elkwater townsite, you'll find Elkwater Lake Lodge and Resort as well as a few shops and restaurants.

The Alberta side of the park is a year-round recreational wonderland. Summer activities include hiking and cycling on more than 50 kilometres of trails, wildlife watching, birding, frisbee golf, mini-golf and water activities. There are two designated swimming areas

with sandy beaches, a food concession and playground facilities.

In the winter, there are over 40 kilometres of groomed cross-country ski trails, a snow slide, a toboggan hill, an ice-skating trail, an outdoor hockey rink, a downhill ski resort, fat-biking (also called snow-biking) trails, snowshoe trails and other winter events. The visitor centre rents skis, skates, snowshoes and kick sleds in winter and fishing gear, canoes, kayaks, paddle-boards, paddleboats, bikes and child cabooses in summer. Guided nature walks and other interpretive programs can also be booked at the visitor centre.

## West Block

About 55 kilometres south of Maple Creek, Saskatchewan, this area of the park is full of backcountry charm. Two rustic campgrounds and an equestrian campground complete with corrals and stalls make good bases for further exploration into this wilderness area.

The Conglomerate Cliffs and the Hidden Conglomerate Cliffs, which are made up of gravel and stones known as "cobbles," are two highlights of this area. The Conglomerate Cliffs are a short drive from Fort Walsh National Historic Site and offer breathtaking views of the valley and

↑ **Visitors can enjoy easy kayaking on Elkwater Lake in the Alberta section of the park.**

**↑ The log buildings found today at Fort Walsh were designed to evoke the original fort, which was abandoned in 1883.**

**↗ The Conglomerate Cliffs are a breathtaking attraction in West Block.**

whiskey traders took part in the mass murder of a peaceful camp of Assiniboine people. The Cypress Hills Massacre led to the creation of the North-West Mounted Police (NWMP) and the establishment of Fort Walsh.

Visiting the Fort Walsh National Historic Site in West Block is an opportunity to step back in time, to the 1870s, and discover what life was like for the young police officers who first worked in the area. Visitors to the fort can see re-enactments of the NWMP marching on parade in scarlet serge, listen to Métis traditional stories and learn traditional crafts.

tree-covered slopes as well as great birdwatching opportunities. The Hidden Conglomerate Cliffs can only be accessed by a multi-use trail that is part of the Great Trail (formerly the Trans-Canada Trail). The road and the trail to the cliffs are not accessible in extremely wet conditions.

## Fort Walsh National Historic Site

The Cypress Hills area has a long history with Indigenous Peoples, including the Cree, Assiniboine, Atsina, Blackfoot, Saulteaux, Sioux, Crow and others. On June 1, 1873, a group of American bison hunters, wolfers, Métis cargo haulers and American and Canadian

## Centre Block

Most of the facilities on the Saskatchewan side of the park can be found in Centre Block, a 20-minute drive south from Maple Creek. The visitor centre, park administration, Cypress Park Resort Inn and five main campgrounds with over 600 sites can be found here. There are 27 kilometres of hiking trails that can be explored on foot, by mountain bike or on a guided Segway tour. Winter visitors can enjoy 16 kilometres of groomed cross-country ski trails, an outdoor hockey rink and designated snowmobile trails. Cross-country ski rentals are available.

From June to September, you can join a guided hike led by park interpretive staff or participate in other scheduled kid-friendly programming. Families particularly enjoy the sandy beach along the shoreline of Loch Leven. There is a playground, a designated swimming area and change rooms/washroom facilities right at the beach. Boat rentals, horseshoe pits and a beach volleyball court are right next door. Serious swimmers will want to check out the outdoor Cypress Hills Leisure Pool.

Visiting the Cypress Hills Observatory is another highlight of this park. Cypress Hills Interprovincial Park is a designated dark sky preserve and an evening visit to the observatory is a great way to learn more about astronomy and the night sky. You might even locate a new celestial body. In 2001 an amateur astronomer named Vance Petriew attended the Saskatchewan Summer Star Party in Cypress Hills, which takes place every August, and discovered a comet. The comet was officially named Comet Petriew (P/2001 Q2) after its discoverer.

↑ **The annual Saskatchewan Summer Star Party is a great way to take advantage of Cypress Hill's breathtaking skies.**

# Grasslands National Park

by Jenn Smith Nelson

**Sleep in a teepee, howl with coyotes and experience true conservation in action in the only national park featuring prairie grasslands**

## What Makes This Hot Spot Hot?

- Several rare and endangered native species have been reintroduced into the area.
- Hikers can explore a valley once dominated by dinosaurs.
- The Ecotour Scenic Drive takes visitors past interesting landforms, animal colonies and more.

**Address:** East Block Visitor Centre (McGowan Visitor Centre): Waverley No. 44, Fir Mountain, SK
West Block Visitor Centre: 101 Centre St, Val Marie, SK
**GPS:**
East Block: 49.07136; −106.52961
West Block: 49.245769; −107.732181
**Tel.:** East Block: (306) 476-2018
West Block: (877) 345-2257
**Website:** www. pc.gc.ca/en /pn-np/sk/grasslands/index

**Open year-round**

**&#9855; (Limited, check ahead)**

There may be no better place in Saskatchewan to enjoy the province's iconic wide-open prairie space than Grasslands National Park. It's arguably Saskatchewan's best spot to witness the "Land of Living Skies" by night, as it is one of Canada's darkest Dark Sky Preserves. It's also the only national park to represent the prairie grasslands natural region.

Created by erosion from glacial meltwater, the park features a mix of open grasslands, stunning buttes, rolling hills, coulees and the scenic vistas of the Frenchman River Valley. Its plains are also littered with unique land formations and jam-packed with rare flora and a mix of water, land and sky critters.

The plains bison, the swift fox and the black-footed ferret are among the endangered native species that have been reintroduced into the area. Grasslands National Park is

also home to 30 at-risk species. Resident mammals, such as badgers, coyotes and pronghorn antelopes, and reptiles, including prairie rattlesnakes, can be spotted throughout the park. Dusk and dawn are the best times of day to look for fauna, as there isn't a lot of respite from the sun, especially during scorching summer days.

The park is a year-round birdwatching hot spot. Look for spotted towhees in riparian shrubs, rock wrens in the badlands and golden eagles in the buttes. Year-round residents like the endangered greater sage-grouse and sharp-tailed grouse are best viewed in spring, while summer provides the perfect chance to see the vulnerable long-billed curlews, longspurs and Sprague's pipits.

Stop at the visitor centres to learn about the variety of events, self-guided tours and interpretive and junior naturalist programs in the park. Many activities are available, from geocaching, mountain biking (note: there are no designated trails) and horseback riding to paddling.

Between the park's two blocks, you'll find diverse activities that make each area an excellent choice to explore in its own right. As the current park holdings are over 700 square kilometres, plan ahead, and take your time touring these incredible grasslands over several days or trips.

## East Block

Get your hands dirty digging for fossils in the badlands of East Block. Much like nearby Eastend, the eroding layers

↑ The eroded buttes and exposed badland formations found in East Block are ruggedly beautiful.

← Plains bison were reintroduced to the park in December 2005.

↓ The endangered greater short-horned lizard is a master of camouflage.

of earth are dense with 65-million-year-old (and older) fossils of dinosaurs and ancient sea dwellers. Guided digs take place during annual summer events centred on fossil discovery.

Hikers can choose from four front-country hiking trails, ranging from 1 to 8 kilometres one way. They include the Creek to Peak Trail, Rock Creek Trail and Red Buttes Trail.

One outstanding trek that's popular with experienced hikers is the Valley of 1,000 Devils. Take in the landscape of striped red-clay hoodoos while roaming the 800-hectare badlands, where dinosaurs once dominated. This trail is rated difficult and is 12 kilometres out and back. Keep an eye out for patches of quicksand (yes, really!) and the greater short-horned lizard. If you are very lucky, you may spot these endangered reptiles in the badland habitat.

East Block is home to the McGowan Visitor Centre (open May long weekend to Thanksgiving), and within Rock Creek Campground, there are a good number of front-country camping options. In addition to 24 tent and RV sites, cool Parks Canada accommodations include eight oTENTiks (a cross between a tent and a cabin) and three teepees. There are no designated backcountry sites, though backcountry camping is permitted.

Visit the Parks Canada website for information on what to expect, and register in person at the visitor centre prior to setting out on your backcountry adventure.

## West Block

If you've happened upon a bison roadblock, you've entered the West Block. In addition to incredible landscapes and archaeologically significant sites, West Block is chock full of wildlife. The best way to take it all in is with the Ecotour Scenic Drive — a 2.5 hour, 80-kilometre self-guided drive along Ecotour Road. Historical homesteads, important archaeological sites, interesting land formations, animal colonies and a rubbing stone are all stops to explore during the driving tour.

One of the cutest (and noisiest) stops is at a black-tailed prairie dog colony. Grasslands National Park and the adjacent lands are the only places where they live in Canada. Here, quirky antics and the sophisticated chirps of these native prairie dwellers reign supreme. Endangered burrowing owls can often be spotted on or near the colonies, as they take over abandoned burrows.

West Block boasts 11 front-country hiking trails that offer a variety of views and focal points. Over 12,000 ancient

↑ **Black-tailed prairie dogs are a keystone species, as their population health affects numerous other species.**

↑↑ **The teepee accommodations in West Block offer panoramic views of the open prairie and rolling hills.**

teepee rings are scattered throughout the park, and you can hike the easy 2-kilometre Tipi Ridge Trail loop to view a few of them. For those who want to get to know the park's flora, Eagle Butte Trail showcases both common and rare species along a moderate 2.1-kilometre loop. A favourite of bison, blue grama grass is quite easy to find on this trail, as are needle-and-thread grass and prickly pear cacti. Plant lovers should also look for gumbo evening primrose, with flowers that change colour in the evenings. For those who are up for a challenge, the hike to 70 Mile Butte will not disappoint. This 4.1-kilometre loop guides hikers to one of the highest points in the park and offers spectacular views.

Like East Block, there are many types of accommodations in the scenic Frenchman River Campground, which delivers views of the river, rolling hills and, sometimes, even bison. There are 20 electrical front-country camping sites and four oTENTiks. Teepee rentals are also available at the Two Trees day-use area. Several designated sites for backcountry camping also exist in West Block. All reservations can be made online or at the visitor centre, which is open early May to Thanksgiving.

Equestrian camping with access to water, horse pens and more is also available in both blocks. In West Block, equestrian sites can be found south of the Belza day-use area, and in East Block, sites are found in Rock Creek Campground.

↑ The hike to 70 Mile Butte is one of the best spots in the park to take in the sunset.

# Chaplin Lake

by Jenn Smith Nelson

*With over 100,000 shorebirds arriving each spring, including up to half of the world's sanderlings, this is one of the most important bird migration points in the country*

## What Makes This Hot Spot Hot?

- Chaplin Lake is the second-largest saline lake in Canada.
- Over 30 species of shorebirds visit Chaplin annually, including plovers, avocets, sandpipers and godwits.
- The Chaplin Nature Centre offers a wealth of information on shorebirds and guided tours.

**Address:** Off the Trans-Canada Hwy (Hwy 1), near Chaplin, SK
**GPS:** 50.4566; –106.65952
**Tel.:** (306) 395-2770
**Website:** www.chaplintourism.com

**Open early May to early September**

&#x267F; (Limited, check ahead)

↗ **A large variety of shorebirds gather and intermingle in the saline waters.**

Bordering the rural village of Chaplin, along the Trans-Canada Highway, the 20-square-kilometre Chaplin Lake is the second-largest saline water body in Canada and, in season, is jam packed with migratory birds.

Besides being a source of high-quality sodium sulphate (the white stuff you see along the road), the lake is a significant shorebird-nesting habitat. In 1997 it was designated a site of hemispheric importance, the highest designation possible by the Western Hemisphere Shorebird Reserve Network (WHSRN). To merit this designation, a site must host at least 500,000 shorebirds annually or 30 per cent of the population of a single species, and Chaplin is one of only three such sites in Canada.

Each year thousands of visitors and hundreds of birders flock to Chaplin Lake, hoping to add to their life list from the over 30 species of shorebirds that visit the sandy marshlands. Which bird tops the most-wanted list? Most often, it's the endangered piping plover. One-third of the population of this at-risk species is found in Canada, with Saskatchewan noted as

a major nesting area for the small birds.

Other notable seasonal visitors include at times up to half the world's population of sanderlings, stunningly marked American avocets, stilt sandpipers, marbled godwits and killdeer.

Mid-May is the optimal time for visiting, when birds that pit stop in Chaplin come by the thousands, with some returning in August and September followed by their young. Many, such as the plovers, come to nest. Others, like sanderlings and semipalmated sandpipers, come to fuel up en route to their Arctic breeding grounds. This pattern has repeated for thousands of years, and with so few predators in the area to be concerned about, they can fatten up in peace in preparation for their next long haul. In a fluster of intermingled avian activity, shorebirds feast on brine shrimp, brine flies and insects found along the salty shores and shallow waters.

Though shorebirds are the star attraction, other exceptional and threatened bird species can be spotted amid the surrounding prairie land, including burrowing owls, ferruginous hawks and long-billed curlews.

You can do a self-guided tour, but it's limited to one stretch of road along Highway 58. Due to private roads with restricted access, your best bet is to take a guided tour of the lake's best vantage points, which provide up-close viewing of the birds and their nesting areas. Tours can be booked through the Chaplin Nature Centre.

If you continue 20 minutes west along the Trans-Canada Highway to Reed Lake, also part of the WHSRN-designated area, you'll find a viewing tower just west of Morse that allows you to scan the bird-filled landscape from above.

↑ The wind kicks up clouds of salt along a sodium-sulphate-lined private road, which can only be accessed through guided tours.

↓↓ American avocets are easy to spot at Chaplin Lake.

↓ The piping plover, a species at risk, nests along Chaplin Lake.

# The Great Sandhills

by Jenn Smith Nelson

**One of Canada's largest sets of active sand dunes, this somewhat hidden land formation is definitely worth seeking out**

## What Makes This Hot Spot Hot?

- The dunes measure over 15 metres high in places.
- Over 150 bird species and 20 types of mammals can be spotted here.
- The dunes are the perfect environment for the endangered Ord's kangaroo rat, which nests in the area.

**Address:** Turn south on the first grid road west of Sceptre, off Hwy 32, and then drive about 22 km south to the Great Sandhills; watch for signs and a parking lot
**GPS:** 50.69368; –109.28238
**Tel.:** (306) 623-4345
**Website:** www.greatsandhills museum.com

**Open year-round, weather permitting**

↗ **Boot Hill greets you from the parking lot.**

For those who have never been to Saskatchewan, a desert-like habitat existing in the middle of the Prairies might be hard to fathom. However, the sand dunes that make up the Great Sandhills, in Saskatchewan's southwest, are among the country's largest and most active. Protected within the Great Sandhills Ecological Reserve, sand-covered hills tower above an impressive 1,900 square kilometres of terrain. Thanks to wind, this desert-type terrain is perpetually shifting and changing.

Accessing the dunes can be tricky (you might need to ask for directions at the Great Sandhills Museum in Sceptre), but once you've found the parking lot with trail signage directing you up the dunes, you've arrived. Before spotting the sand, you'll be greeted by "Boot Hill," a unique and charming gateway covered in boots made by local rancher John Both (now passed). Ranching has long occurred in the area, so don't be surprised if you see or hear cattle.

The trail to the dunes is spotted from Boot Hill, and a 500-metre walk will get you to the top of the closest dune.

Once on the dunes, kick off your shoes and feel the surprisingly soft sand between your toes. Don't underestimate the difficulty of hiking along the trails and on top of the soft sand dunes. If you are up

for the challenge, head for the longer dunes found just east of Boot Hill.

While navigating the mounds, look for native grasses, such as sagebrush, along with stunted shrubs that cling to life. Some aspen, birch and even willow trees surround the area.

Many mammals commonly found in Saskatchewan's southwest, like coyotes, foxes, weasels, porcupines, pronghorn antelopes and both mule and white-tailed deer, inhabit the area. There's also some rare wildlife hidden in the dunes. The endangered Ord's kangaroo rat nests in the area, requiring sparsely vegetated and actively eroding sand dunes for its habitat. While in the area, bird enthusiasts can look for the fittingly named sandhill crane as well as short-eared owls and peregrine falcons.

The massive reserve offers simple but beautiful vistas that stretch for kilometres. Saskatchewan's big sky as the backdrop against the expanse of sand makes for fabulous photos, so it's worth bringing your phone or camera along for the trek.

Bear in mind it's easy to get turned around in the Great Sandhills, so bring a compass along. This area doesn't have bathrooms, and camping and fires aren't permitted. You should also avoid the area if it's raining, as the dirt roads leading to the site can be difficult to pass.

↑ The desert-like terrain makes you feel like you are far from Saskatchewan.

↓ Hard to spot because they are tiny (and nocturnal), the rare Ord's kangaroo rat nests in the sand dunes.

# Little Manitou Lake

by Jenn Smith Nelson

**Be literally unsinkable in Canada's Dead Sea**

## What Makes This Hot Spot Hot?

- Little Manitou Lake is one of only three lakes in the world where the water is saturated with mineral salts.
- The water has healing and therapeutic properties, and salts and mud from the lake are used in spa treatments.
- Nearby hiking trails connect the tranquil Wellington Park to the area's campground.

**Address:** Manitou Beach, SK
**GPS:** 51.72091; –105.44457
**Tel.:** (866) 756-6665
**Website:** www.watrousmanitou.com

**Open June to August**

&#9855; **(Limited, check ahead)**

↗ **Floating is so easy in Canada's Dead Sea that you can read a book while taking a dip.**

Often called Canada's Dead Sea, Little Manitou Lake is found within the resort village of Manitou Beach, located between Regina and Saskatoon. Unique in the western hemisphere, the lake is known for its salinity and healing properties.

So what exactly characterizes water with salt levels that are three times more concentrated than ocean water? Buoyancy! Those who enter the water can float with ease — lay back, read a book or visit with friends while suspended effortlessly near the surface.

As an endorheic (terminal) basin, the lake doesn't have constant flow to or from rivers and streams. It remains calm and uninterrupted for long periods, and over time the lake's salinity increases as water evaporates. The water, dense with minerals, eventually reaches a point where it can no longer hold salt in a dissolved state.

This 22.5-kilometre-long and 1.6-kilometre-wide lake has long been celebrated. The lake was named *Manitou* by settlers, Algonquian for "Great Spirit," because of its mysterious qualities. For centuries Indigenous Peoples have visited these sacred mineral-rich waters to take advantage of the lake's many health benefits.

Today the lake is also a sought-after tourist destination — for the same reason. Not only is it amusing, floating effortlessly in the water, but the minerals from the lake offer an all-natural therapeutic experience that attracts visitors from far and wide.

From healing sunburns to providing relief from conditions such as arthritis and psoriasis, the water, with its buoyancy and density of sodium, magnesium and potassium salts, can help those with chronic ailments. The water is also known to help boost the immune system and even tighten skin.

Both salt and mud from Little Manitou Lake are used in spa treatments at the local Manitou Springs Resort and Mineral Spa. The lake's beneficial water can also be found in the resort's indoor mineral pools, which are open year-round.

While in the area, hike the Manitou Beach Trails. The well-groomed trails (3.5-kilometre and 5-kilometre loops) can be accessed from Manitou and District Regional Park campground and will lead you through Wellington Park, a tranquil area with a bubbling stream. There you can spot wildlife, such as mule and white-tailed deer, shorebirds and waterfowl.

⬆ **The sun sets over Little Manitou Lake.**

# Wanuskewin Heritage Park

by Jenn Smith Nelson

**Impactful, authentic cultural experiences can be found at this Indigenous meeting place, where visitors can connect with nature**

## What Makes This Hot Spot Hot?

- Wanuskewin is Canada's longest-running archaeological dig site.
- Four interpretive trails allow hikers to experience both the cultural and natural wonders of the area.
- Visitors can enjoy a teepee sleepover and engaging workshops while learning all about traditional Indigenous living.

**Address:** RR 4, Penner Rd, Saskatoon, SK
**GPS:** 52.22427; –106.59605
**Tel.:** (306) 931-6767
**Website:** www.wanuskewin.com

**Open year-round**

&#9855; **(Check ahead)**

↗ **Explore the mixed-grassland region surrounding Wanuskewin Heritage Park.**

You don't always have to go far to discover something new, or in this case something very old. By travelling a mere 5 kilometres outside of Saskatoon's city limits, visitors will be transported to a place where connectivity with nature and immersion in Indigenous history and culture go hand in hand.

It is estimated that humans have been gathering at Wanuskewin for the past 6,000 years. This spot was likely chosen by Indigenous Peoples of the Northern Plains because of its topography. It is quite different from surrounding areas — with steep cliffs for buffalo jumps, access to water and shelter from the prairie wind. Archaeological digs have been taking place at the park's site since the 1980s. This excavation project is led by the park's founder, Dr. Ernie Walker, and it is the longest-running continuous dig site in Canada.

The park features 19 precontact sites, including two buffalo jumps. Bones and objects found here are thousands of years old, with many of the archaeological finds predating Egypt's pyramids. During the spring and summer months, visitors can take part in tours and witness active excavations. Guided dig site tours take place

May through August. The park also showcases a medicine wheel, teepee rings and more, uncovering the day-to-day traditions of the Indigenous Peoples of the Northern Plains.

Wanuskewin is set above the Opimihaw Creek and South Saskatchewan River, in a moist mixed-grassland ecoregion. You can best explore the area by walking in the footsteps of ancient ancestors along four pathways and 6 kilometres of trails. The trails are available for exploration during any season. Keep an eye out for over 100 species of wildlife, such as beavers, coyotes, rabbits and birds that inhabit the area.

The park's evolving programming allows visitors to discover its rich past and present. In addition to hiking, activities such as teepee building, traditional games, workshops, crafts and dance performances help visitors connect with the region's natural and cultural environments.

Wanuskewin, designated a National Historic Site in 1986, has made the UNESCO World Heritage Site tentative list and it's hoped it will become the first World Heritage Site in Saskatchewan. A plan to reintroduce bison to the park is planned for early 2020.

↑ A trio of bronze bison greet visitors near the front entrance. Two buffalo jumps have been discovered on the park's site.

# Redberry Lake Biosphere Reserve

by Jenn Smith Nelson

*An ecologically significant region for many migrating bird species, this reserve promotes sustainability and conservation*

## What Makes This Hot Spot Hot?

- Redberry Lake is designated both an Important Bird Area and a Migratory Bird Sanctuary.
- The reserve provides habitats for nine endangered, threatened or rare bird species and over 180 other bird species.
- There are five hiking trails and plenty of recreational opportunities around Redberry Lake.

**Address:** Hwy 40, 12.8 km east of Hafford, SK
**GPS:** 52.71241; –107.21499
**Tel.:** (306) 549-2360
**Website:** www.redberrylake.ca

**Open year-round; the regional park is open May 1 to September 30**

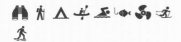

&#x267F; **(Check ahead)**

The UNESCO-designated Redberry Lake Biosphere Reserve is the only one of its kind in Saskatchewan and one of just 18 designated biosphere reserves in Canada. An important conservation area, it's a wonderful place to discover native plants and animals.

Over 112,000-plus hectares of lakes, marshes, rolling hills and aspen groves make up the reserve, along with small patches of natural mixed prairie, which is rare in this part of Saskatchewan. Prairie grasses, like fescue, sedge and wheat grass, can be found along with aspen and shrubs, such as gooseberry, hawthorn, raspberry, silver buffalo berry and silver willow. Lakeside in the uplands, rolling hills feature beaked hazel, dogwood, saskatoon berry and chokecherry shrubs.

The saline Redberry Lake is a haven for wildlife, and as a Migratory Bird Sanctuary, this area is protected. Four islands

on the closed-basin, flat-bottomed lake mark an important breeding ground and staging point for both waterfowl and shorebirds. Visitors are not permitted on the islands between April 15 and September 15 so as not to disrupt nesting birds. An estimated 30,000 ducks, tundra swans and geese eat and rest here during migration seasons.

Over 180 species have been recorded, including common water-loving species (such as American white pelicans and American avocets), many types of warblers (chestnut-sided, Canada, Tennessee and

more) and nine endangered, threatened or rare bird species (Sprague's pipits, loggerhead shrikes, California gulls and white-winged scoters, among others). Additionally, piping plovers nest along Redberry's sandy beaches, and the reserve is also along the migration route of one of North America's most endangered birds, the whooping crane. Fall is a great time to visit to witness birds migrating south as the area is quiet, although amenities are not available.

Besides birdwatching, hiking is a popular activity in the area. The intermediate 1.5-kilometre Lookout Trail features fabulous lake views, while the moderately rated 2-kilometre Grassland Golf Course Walking Trail showcases a variety of vegetation, from aspen woods to mixed grasses. An abundance of red-berry bushes can be found along the easy 3.4-kilometre Millennium Point Hiking Trail, which has interpretive signage and a raised platform overlooking the marsh. Check ahead to ensure the platform is open as it has been flooded out in the past.

The summer months offer opportunities for swimming and water sports in Redberry Lake and fishing in the nearby trout pond, which is found in Redberry Lake Regional Park. There are 148 campsites in the regional park, and camping is available between May 1 and September 30. The quietness and remoteness of the reserve draws in cross-country skiers and snowshoers in the winter.

↑ **Views of Redberry Lake.**

← **Listed as a vulnerable species, Sprague's pipit has been recorded in the area.**

# Prince Albert National Park

by Jenn Smith Nelson

**The meeting of lowlands and uplands provides an ecologically diverse area for those seeking a mix of wildlife watching, outdoor adventure and camping**

## What Makes This Hot Spot Hot?

- The national park is home to a protected American white pelican colony that is Canada's second-largest breeding colony.
- Free-range plains bison can be spotted in the park.
- Hikers and paddlers can undertake the iconic trek to Grey Owl's Cabin.

**Address:** 969 Lakeview Dr., Waskesiu Lake, SK
**GPS:** 53.94696; –106.3888
**Tel.:** (306) 663-4522
**Website:** www.pc.gc.ca/en /pn-np/sk/princealbert/index

**Open year-round**

&#9855; (Check ahead)

One of two national parks in Saskatchewan, Prince Albert National Park spans 3,875 square kilometres of protected land, where enchanting boreal forest meets aspen parkland. With an incredible landscape designed by ancient glaciers, the park is 30 per cent water and rich in forests, spruce bogs and even rare fescue grasslands.

It offers a good mix of accessibility and remoteness, which makes it a popular destination for those seeking active outdoor adventures. The hardest thing when visiting Prince Albert National Park is deciding what to do first.

The visitor centre, found across from the main beach area in the town of Waskesiu Lake, is open daily year-round and is the best place to gather information and make your plans. It offers plenty of cultural and nature-oriented interactive displays and programming to keep you busy throughout the day. Take time to visit the centre to learn about the full range of activities in the park.

The town site of Waskesiu Lake is set within the heart of the park and attracts many who choose to stay in the area. It's an ideal hub from which to set out exploring, and it has a variety of accommodation offerings, such as campgrounds, cabins, oTENTiks (which are a cross between a tent and a cabin) and more. For those seeking quieter areas, the park has 12 designated backcountry campgrounds.

The town also provides easy access to the lake bearing the same name and its 600-metre-long beach. This area draws scores of people who spend long summer days enjoying the beach, picnic facilities and a nearby nature-themed playground. Many visitors also partake in water sports, ranging from canoeing and kayaking to stand-up paddleboarding, wakeboarding and waterskiing. In the winter, the lake draws adrenaline junkies for kiteskiing and kiteboarding across the icy waters. The site is perfect for both sports thanks to Saskatchewan's notoriously fierce wind gusts.

During the summer, anglers can head to one of the three largest lakes — Crean, Kingsmere or Waskesiu — to try to reel in the area's most wanted: walleye, whitefish, suckers and northern pike. In the winter, anglers can go ice fishing on Waskesiu Lake. Ice shacks are permitted (but must be removed each night); however, vehicles are not allowed on the ice. The winter season is open until March 31.

Hiking is one of Prince Albert's biggest attractions, with over 17 trails (and multiple loops within trails) spanning the park. Each of the trails possesses unique attributes, but nearly all offer breathtaking panoramas, lush vegetation and numerous points of interest. From

marshes and bogs to forested pathways and observation points, choosing even a handful of trails to explore is difficult. Whichever you choose, there are plenty of opportunities to learn about the area's ecology and spot some interesting wildlife.

⬆ The park is one of only a few spots in Canada where plains bison still roam within their historical range.

⬉ The main beach at Waskesiu Lake is a great place for families to spend the day.

↑ **Look for wildlife while hiking the 2-kilometre loop of the Mud Creek Trail.**

↗ **Outdoor adventurers can portage or hike to Grey Owl's Cabin.**

Watch for residents such as foxes, grey wolves, moose, elk, black bears, beavers, lynx and over 200 bird species. The park protects an American white pelican colony, which happens to be Canada's second-largest breeding colony. The pelicans are found on Heron Island, on Lavallée Lake in the park's northwest corner. This area also supports large populations of nesting double-crested cormorants and ring-billed gulls.

Prince Albert National Park is also home to a herd of plains bison. In fact, it's one of only a few herds in Canada that is roaming within the species' original historical range. If you come across the herd, exercise caution and keep your distance — after all, plains bison are one of the largest land mammals in North America.

Wildlife enthusiasts should head up Narrows Road to find the Mud Creek Trail, a 2-kilometre loop where both an active beaver lodge and, thanks to spawning fish, black bears can be found. Among the loop's dark spruce and aspen stands, bird species such as warblers, hermit thrush, brown creepers and even ruffed grouse can be spotted. Many visitors enjoy the interpretive trails located a short drive from Waskesiu Lake. One favourite excursion is the Boundary Bog Trail, an easy 2-kilometre loop. This tranquil moss-covered trail features many black spruce bogs.

For the adventurous, the park's most iconic trek, the

Grey Owl Trail, provides an opportunity to hike to the cabin of Englishman Archibald Stansfeld Belaney. Belaney was a conservationist who was better known by his chosen name, Grey Owl. This 40-kilometre round-trip hike is rated intermediate and accessed through the Kingsmere day-use area. The trail follows the eastern shore of Kingsmere Lake. Hikers pass through bogs and meadows, forest and back-country campgrounds before arriving at Grey Owl's Cabin, named "Beaver Lodge," where it's rumoured he bunked with his pet beavers. Many canoeists and kayakers also portage to the cabin following the route along the eastern shoreline of the lake.

In the winter, strap on snowshoes or cross-country skis to enjoy lake views while exploring Waskesiu Lake's beach area. Prefer groomed trails? The Fisher Trail (a 6.3-kilometre loop) can be accessed from the town or, for a longer route, choose the Crean Lake Trail (which is 19 kilometres return).

Wildlife viewing in the park is optimal when it snows, as it's easy to spot fresh tracks on the roads. Drive the Narrows Road and chances are high that you'll witness elk nipping balsam buds in snowy ditches, curious Canada jays flitting about and even otters venturing to and from a nearby lake.

↑ River otters call Prince Albert home year-round and are said to delight in the frigid temperatures.

↑↑ Elk are commonly spotted within the park.

# Spruce Woods Provincial Park

by Doug O'Neill

*The presence of the northern prairie skink, Manitoba's only native lizard, can be surprising, but so too are the towering desert-like sand dunes*

## What Makes This Hot Spot Hot?

- The park is home to the Spirit Sands, the only set of sand dunes in all of Manitoba.
- A beautiful blue-green pond called the Devil's Punch Bowl was formed by underground streams eroding and collapsing the hills.
- Manitoba's only native lizard, the northern prairie skink, hangs out on the grassy hillsides.

**Address:** Provincial Trunk Hwy 5, 29 km south of the Trans-Canada Hwy (Hwy 1)
**GPS:** 49.66239; –99.26687
**Tel.:** (888) 482-2267
**Website:** www.gov.mb.ca /sd/parks/park-maps-and -locations/western/spruce.html

**Open year-round**

&#x267F; (Check ahead)

&#x2197; **Spirit Sands, a 4-square-kilometre tract of sand, is like no other landform in Manitoba.**

You're ambling through Spruce Woods Provincial Park, and suddenly you come upon a stretch of 30-metre-high sand dunes, pincushion cacti and perhaps one or two hognose snakes. This is Manitoba? You walk another 30 minutes, and the vista changes again. Suddenly an oasis of spruce trees next to a blue-green spring-fed pond comes into view. Such are the contrasts of Spirit Sands and the Devil's Punch Bowl — two diverse habitats within Spruce Woods Provincial Park, 180 kilometres outside Winnipeg.

Spirit Sands is the name of the 4-square-kilometre tract of sand that's like no other landform in Manitoba. It's the only remaining unvegetated area of the Assiniboine Delta, which prompts people to call it a desert, though the area receives nearly twice the amount of precipitation that a true desert does. Back when ancient Lake Agassiz still existed (before it was drained thousands of years ago), the area was covered with 6,500 square kilometres of delta sand. Only these 4 square kilometres remain visible — the rest is now covered by plants and inhabited by wildlife.

A short distance away, the sand slides down a 45-metre depression into a pool of blue-green water known as the Devil's Punch Bowl, which is the result of underground streams eroding and collapsing the hills. Visitors to Spruce Woods Provincial Park can view these curiosities of nature by following the self-guided Spirit Sands/Devil's Punch Bowl Trail. The trail has boardwalks and stairs, so visitors can tour the area and

minimize disturbance to the sand and vegetation.

Spruce Woods Provincial Park also encompasses spruce parkland (hence its name), upland deciduous forest and mixed-grass prairie within its 269 square kilometres. Wildlife varies depending on the section of the park. White-tailed deer make their home in the parkland, while ruffed grouse, raccoons and various species of weasels are drawn to the lush riverbanks. In spring and summer, you may spot a surprising species scuttling across the ground in Spruce Woods. The northern prairie skink, the only lizard native to Manitoba, is found in areas with sandy soil and mixed-grass prairie vegetation. The skink spends more than seven months of the year hibernating underground and requires the park's sandy soil for its winter burrow.

Nature lovers can bed down at Kiche Manitou campground (which has 200 campsites) or head to one of the five designated hike-in camping sites along the Epinette Creek Trails. (A note to campers: it is illegal to use or transport disease-carrying elm firewood.)

Friends of Spruce Woods Provincial Park operate the Spirit Sands Interpretive Centre and the Spirit Sands Museum. Volunteers lead interpretive tours throughout the summer. Other activities at the park include canoeing, swimming, hiking, horseback riding and biking. However, cyclists should note that, for environmental reasons, bikes are not allowed on the Spirit Sands/Devil's Punch Bowl, Isputinaw, Marsh Lake and Spring Ridge Trails.

↑ Sand slides down a 45-metre depression into a pool of blue-green water known as the Devil's Punch Bowl.

↓ In spring and summer, the northern prairie skink is typically found in areas with sandy soil and mixed-grass prairie vegetation.

# Whiteshell Provincial Park

by Doug O'Neill

*This 2,721-square-kilometre park is home to Manitoba's deepest lake, a glacially carved pond that gets covered over with lilies each summer and a world-class goose sanctuary*

## What Makes This Hot Spot Hot?

- With Canadian Shield, boreal forests, sandy beaches, rock ridges and bogs, there's no shortage of protected parkland to explore.
- West Hawk Lake, Manitoba's deepest lake, is popular with scuba divers.
- Each fall, over 1,000 Canada geese prepare for fall migration at the Alfred Hole Goose Sanctuary.

**Address:** 130 km east of Winnipeg, MB; follow the Trans-Canada Hwy (Hwy 1) or Provincial Trunk Hwy 44
**GPS:** 49.74585; −95.21349
**Tel.:** (866) 626-4862
**Website:** www.whiteshell.mb.ca

**Open year-round; Alfred Hole's visitor centre is open May until Thanksgiving**

Note that flooding and high water levels may affect access to the park's trails. Please check local conditions before planning a visit.

♿ (Limited, check ahead)

Located close to the Manitoba-Ontario border, Whiteshell Provincial Park comprises 2,721 square kilometres of protected wilderness parkland, which includes about 200 lakes, rushing rivers, rugged Canadian Shield, boreal forests, ancient rock ridges, sandy beaches and bogs.

A crashing meteorite gets the credit for creating one of the more surprising visitor activities in Whiteshell Provincial Park: scuba diving at West Hawk Lake. The impact of the meteorite resulted in the deepest lake in Manitoba, at 115 metres. Geologists estimate that the crater at the bottom of the lake could be 100 million years old.

Hundreds of kilometres of trails cater to hikers (and, in the winter, skiers and snowshoers) of all levels. Experienced hikers gravitate to the Mantario Trail, a 60-kilometre hike through Canadian Shield. Paddlers have 325 kilometres of canoe routes to explore. The 170-kilometre Caddy Lake Canoe Route takes canoeists through rock tunnels blasted out of granite during railroad construction in the early 1900s.

Legions of plant lovers visit Lily Pond (on Highway 44, west of Caddy Lake) during the summer months, when the pond is blanketed with white and yellow lilies.

There's plenty of wildlife to spot, some more elusive than others: wolves, white-tailed deer, moose, turkey vultures and otters, to name a handful. Black bears inhabit the park, which means visitors must adhere to Bear Smart safety guidelines. There's also no shortage of species to draw birdwatchers year-round. Chickadees, Canada and blue jays, pine and evening grosbeaks, redpolls, woodpeckers and owls are all found here. Bald eagles and ruby-throated hummingbirds make appearances in summer.

Petroforms, sometimes called boulder mosaics, are found at various sites throughout the park, such as Bannock Point. Anishinaabe and other Indigenous Peoples describe how, thousands of years ago, the rocks were laid out on

the bedrock in the shapes of humans, fish, snakes and turtles as part of teaching and healing ceremonies.

## Alfred Hole Goose Sanctuary

One day in the spring of 1939, mink rancher Alfred Hole rescued four baby Canada geese on his property near Rennie, about a 2-hour drive east of Winnipeg.

Unfazed at the prospect of raising geese, the mink rancher housed the goslings in a pen, fed them dandelions and gave them full run of his pond. Later that season, Hole acquired a gander, which mated with one of the females, and soon after more eggs were laid and hatched. Come autumn, the geese migrated southward, but they returned the following spring.

By the time Hole died in 1959, he had established — with the support of private groups, individuals and the Ministry of Natural Resources — a full-fledged goose sanctuary that's become one of the key attractions at Whiteshell Provincial Park. Currently, hundreds of Canada geese return each spring to the sanctuary to hatch their goslings.

The ideal time to admire the goslings is mid-May to July. To observe the iconic V-shaped flying formations as the geese head south, visit late August to October.

During the summer months, staff at the interpretive centre can teach you about the history of the Canada goose, the aerodynamics of their V-formations and their social habits.

↑ West Hawk Lake, in the heart of Whiteshell Provincial Park, is the deepest lake in Manitoba, reaching a depth of 115 metres in places.

↓ Many Canada geese return to the Alfred Hole Goose Sanctuary each spring to hatch new generations of goslings.

# Oak Hammock Marsh

by Doug O'Neill

**_Visitors will learn the true value of marshlands, which are too often underappreciated_**

## What Makes This Hot Spot Hot?

- Oak Hammock Marsh is one of the most productive ecosystems in Canada, unrivalled in its species diversity.
- There are over 300 species of birds found here.
- The well-equipped interpretive centre offers a wide range of hands-on nature workshops and educational programming.

**Address:** 1 Snow Goose Bay (off Provincial Rd 220), Stonewall, MB
**GPS:** 50.17382; −97.13295
**Tel.:** (888) 506-2774
**Website:** www.oakhammockmarsh.ca

**Open year-round; extended hours from Thursdays to Sundays between mid-September and mid-October for fall migration**

&#9855; **(Check ahead)**

↗ **The yellow warbler is just one of the 300 species of birds that inhabit this 20-square-kilometre stretch of open wetland.**

In the 1890s, the 470-square-kilometre area of marsh and fen near the southwestern corner of Lake Winnipeg was known as St. Andrew's Bog. Not a very romantic name, but back then marshlands weren't appreciated as the gems of nature that they are. Marshlands were to be drained for agricultural purposes. And so they were.

Luckily, thanks to the preservation efforts of Ducks Unlimited Canada and the Manitoba government, 20 square kilometres of open wetland thrive today at what's now called Oak Hammock Marsh. Forward-thinking conservationists constructed 22 kilometres of earth dykes to restore part of the original marsh.

Wetlands, like Oak Hammock Marsh, are among the most productive ecosystems on Earth, second only to rainforests. Such wetlands play an important role in maintaining water quality by filtering sediment and pollutants. They also function as wildlife habitats, store flood waters and maintain surface water flow during dry spells. What looks like a swampy marsh is often the equivalent of a "biological supermarket," acting as a rich food source for numerous species.

Oak Hammock Marsh is home to an incredible diversity of fauna: 300 species of birds; 25 species of mammals; numerous amphibians, reptiles and fish; and countless invertebrates. An excess of 100,000 waterfowl stop at the marsh during their annual migrations, among them snow geese, Canada geese and blue-winged teals. Other birds in transit (some stay for a while) include the yellow rail, Nelson's sparrow and LeConte's sparrow.

Mammals you might spot include squirrels, beavers, rabbits, hares, shrews, deer mice,

foxes, wolves, white-tailed deer, badgers, otters and black bears. Plant life here runs the gamut — from cattails, duckweed, lilies and irises to orchids, willows, dogwood and a wide variety of roses. Fish species include northern pike, white sucker, spottail shiner, common carp, ninespine stickleback, fathead minnow and emerald shiner, to name a few. Fishing is allowed in Oak Hammock Marsh if you have a provincial fishing licence.

There are 30 kilometres of marked trails (gravel paths, wooden boardwalks and earth and grass footpaths), many of which have been constructed on the dykes. The Oak Hammock Interpretive Centre's maps indicate specific areas, such as the squirrel colony, duck

pond and dragonfly area, all of which can be reached on foot.

The interpretive centre offers all manner of educational programs, hands-on workshops and interactive exhibits that emphasize the vital role of marshlands and reveal how they are indeed natural treasures.

↑ Staff at the interpretive centre facilitate educational programs and hands-on workshops to teach visitors about the vital role of marshlands.

↖ The skies over Oak Hammock Marsh are filled with over 100,000 winged creatures during annual migrations.

# Riding Mountain National Park

by Doug O'Neill

***This is one of Canada's most-visited national parks, with 3,000 square kilometres of protected land where bison roam and hundreds of birds and mammal species thrive***

## What Makes This Hot Spot Hot?

- The park, sitting 500 metres above the surrounding prairies, contains three distinct ecosystems: grassland, upland boreal forest and eastern deciduous forest.
- Abundant birdwatching opportunities can be had at serene Lake Katherine.
- Visitors can get up close to one of Canada's few remaining bison herds, at the Lake Audy Bison Enclosure.

**Address:** 133 Wasagaming Dr, Onanole, MB
**GPS:** 50.65757; –99.97232
**Tel.:** (204) 848-7275
**Websites:** www.pc.gc.ca /en/pn-np/riding/index and www.rmbr.ca

**Open year-round; some services and facilities in Wasagaming shut down during the fall and winter**

&#9855; **(Check ahead)**

When it comes to the curative powers of nature, few places rival Riding Mountain National Park. Nature has bestowed unique attributes on the park. Chief among these are the park's three distinct ecosystems: grassland, upland boreal forest and eastern deciduous forest. Distinct plant and animal life thrive in each of these environments. In 1986 UNESCO designated the wilderness park and the surrounding area a Biosphere Reserve.

Riding Mountain is one of only five national parks in Canada with a townsite within its borders: Wasagaming, on the shores of Clear Lake. That's where the Parks Canada office is located and where you might choose to base your exploration of the park.

Wildlife is plentiful. There are more than 233 species of birds, at least 60 kinds of mammals, six types of amphibians and 27 fish species, not to mention 69 species of butterflies. Visitors frequently see moose, beavers, porcupines, white-tailed deer, snowshoe hares and elk. Other creatures, such as cougars, are more elusive. Riding Mountain is home to one of the largest populations of black bears in North America, meaning you should use extra caution when exploring the park. And, of course, there's the Lake Audy Bison Enclosure within the park, which protects a herd of 40 plains bison.

Endangered birds, such as the loggerhead shrike and golden-winged warbler, have surfaced in the park. The trumpeter swan, known for its graceful moves on the water — and rarely seen in Manitoba — nests within the park's boundaries.

Some of the best ways to observe nature include hiking, horseback riding and biking. Fat biking (sometimes referred to as snow biking) has become a popular year-round trail activity, too. There are more than 400 kilometres of hiking and riding trails. Most are clearly marked and easy to follow, while others are better suited for experienced backcountry hikers. Hikers can opt

for one of the relatively easy, self-guided trails that start on the outskirts of Wasagaming, such as the Clear Lake Trail. For those keen to tackle a more challenging hike, there are backcountry trails, such as the 25-kilometre Birdtail Trail in the northwest corner of the park, near Bob Hill Lake.

While many of the services in Wasagaming shut down during winter months, some stay open to cater to visitors who come to snowshoe, cross-country ski and track animals over the snow.

The large campsite at Clear Lake in Wasagaming makes it relatively easy for nature lovers to spend a few days (or longer) in Riding Mountain National Park. For a fully immersive nature experience, check out the various Parks Canada options, from traditional campsites, yurts and Micro-Cubes (a 10-metre-square cube with a panoramic window) to backcountry sites. Riding Mountain also offers a winter camping program.

Other diversions are plentiful and include fishing, boating (check with Parks Canada for any restrictions on motorized boats), kayaking, canoeing, sailing, swimming and scuba diving (especially at Clear Lake).

↑ **Riding Mountain National Park contains three distinct ecosystems, which makes for a huge diversity of flora and fauna and varied panoramas.**

**⬆ Birders will likely hear — sooner than they will see — the evening grosbeak.**

Philadelphia vireos, yellow-rumped warblers, American redstarts, chestnut-sided warblers and boreal chickadees. The elusive Connecticut warbler has also been sighted, as have the Tennessee, Nashville and Cape May warblers. Your birdwatching retreat won't be completely tranquil, though. The evening grosbeak is known to use a variety of sounds to express anger, surprise, fear, pain, curiosity and alarm.

There are a handful of fairly easy, level hiking trails, which are also used by horses. The 2.5-kilometre Loon's Island Trail passes through mature aspen and mixed-wood forests along the east side of the lake. Hikers can easily add on the shorter 1.6-kilometre Evergreen Trail, which loops around the north side.

## Lake Katherine

Solitude, peace and silence are ideal conditions to connect with nature. Apart from the wind rippling through the trembling aspen, there's little noise or drama about Lake Katherine, which was once an active Indigenous settlement. Motorized boats are prohibited on the 27-hectare lake, which is located within the traditional territory of the Anishinaabe Peoples. The firepit and a couple of outdoor structures at the lakeside campground are reminders of the First Nations Interpretive Camp that operated at Lake Katherine until 2000.

The relative calm of the lake makes it easier to spot birds, which are attracted to the surrounding boreal forests: yellow-bellied sapsuckers,

## Lake Audy Bison Enclosure

Within Riding Mountain National Park sits another wildlife treasure: a protected herd of 40 or so plains bison in what's known as the Lake Audy Bison Enclosure, a 500-hectare fenced area that can be toured by vehicle only.

Prior to the arrival of Europeans in North America, plains bison numbered 30 million. A combination of factors, primarily the European demand for furs and the advent of the railway, which brought

↑ **Using viewing platforms, visitors to Lake Audy Bison Enclosure can safely snap a photo of the park's marquis species.**

tens of thousands of settlers into the West, led to the rapid decimation of the bison. By the late 1800s, the massive shaggy brown animals had disappeared from Canada.

In 1931, in an attempt to re-establish bison in Manitoba, a herd of 20 were introduced to the Riding Mountain area. Sadly, bovine tuberculosis, contracted from grazing cows, wiped out the original group. That herd was replaced in 1940 by another 10 bison from Elk Island National Park in Alberta, and the 40 creatures that captivate visitors today are their descendants.

The resident bison roam the enclosure, which is divided into winter and summer pastures. Only visitors in vehicles (private cars or compact tour buses and vans) can tour the entire area. You can exit your vehicle and climb a raised viewing deck where a bison and grasslands exhibit details the natural history of bison and the native grasslands.

In the fall, the Lake Audy Bison Enclosure is an excellent place to observe elk in the wild. Experienced guides will sometimes demonstrate elk bugling on homemade bugles. Real elk bugling, when bull elk call out to each other claiming their territory, heats up during mating season, from late August to late September.

# Little Limestone Lake Provincial Park

by Doug O'Neill

**A touch of the Caribbean in Manitoba thanks to a huge marl lake that changes colour throughout the day**

## What Makes This Hot Spot Hot?

- At 4,000 hectares, Little Limestone Lake is the largest marl lake in the world.
- Limestone cliffs provide excellent winter habitats for bats.
- This park is the only area in Manitoba where four of the province's hoofed creatures share the same habitat.

**Address:** Provincial Trunk Hwy 6, about 60 km north of Grand Rapids, MB
**GPS:** 53.74223; −99.32264
**Tel.:** (888) 482-2267
**Website:**
www. gov.mb.ca/sd/parks

Open year-round; park is non-operational with no facilities

↗ **Little brown bats find hibernacula, or winter habitats, in the park's limestone cliffs, which offer protection from predators.**

Little Limestone Lake Provincial Park, sometimes called "Manitoba's Caribbean" because of the colour of the lake's water, is an IUCN (World Conservation Union) protected area — and for a very good reason: It's the world's largest and most outstanding marl lake. It's also known as Manitoba's "Colour-Changing Lake."

A marl lake changes colour as the temperature of the water rises in summer, causing the calcite in the water to separate and form tiny crystals. This turns the water from clear to an opaque turquoise, surprisingly similar to the waters of the Caribbean Sea. Many visitors have watched this lake's water change from a brilliant turquoise in the morning to a robin's egg blue by the afternoon.

This area is a distinct natural space for another reason: Little brown bats (*Myotis lucifugus*) have discovered excellent winter habitats in caves carved out of the limestone cliffs.

The park is home to an array of species, including songbirds, waterfowl, moose, muskrats, eagles, lynx, foxes and woodland caribou. According to wildlife experts, it also has the distinction of being the only area in Manitoba where four of the province's hoofed animal species share the same habitat: deer, wood

bison, elk and moose. Birders typically spot ring-billed gulls, double-crested cormorants, common terns and various species of ducks and geese, all of which inhabit the lake and shoreline.

The area around the shoreline of Little Limestone Lake is protected, meaning visitors cannot do anything that affects the environment or the area's wildlife. The park itself is non-operational, so there are no camping facilities, boat access sites, roads or marked trails.

↑ Sometimes referred to as Manitoba's "Colour-Changing Lake," Little Limestone Lake is the largest marl lake in the world.

→ The common tern is one of numerous bird species regularly sighted in the park.

# Clearwater Lake Provincial Park

by Doug O'Neill

**Caves, a glacial moraine and some of the deepest (and coldest) waters in Manitoba**

## What Makes This Hot Spot Hot?

- The uncommonly deep Clearwater Lake is 16 kilometres in diameter, taking up almost half the park.
- Visitors can explore dolomite caves that have formed on the shores of Clearwater Lake.
- To the south, visitors can spot the Cusp of The Pas Moraine, one of the most prominent geological formations in Manitoba.

**Address:** Provincial Rd 287, 18 km north of The Pas, MB
**GPS:** 53.99664; –100.95032
**Tel.:** (204) 945-6784
**Website:** www.gov.mb.ca /sd/parks /park-maps-and -locations/northwest /clearwater.html

**Open year-round**

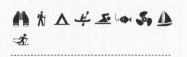

&#9855; **(Check ahead)**

In 2017, Manitobans voted Clearwater Lake the best provincial park in the province — largely because of the lake itself, which takes up almost half of the 593-square-kilometre park.

Clearwater Lake is renowned for its excellent water quality and large lake trout, which thrive in its deep, cool, clear waters, luring anglers from far and wide. The crystalline, circular lake has an average depth of 13.1 metres but gets as deep as 39 metres in places. The reason for such clear water? The lake is spring fed, which means the amount of sediment is minimal compared with lakes fed by rivers and streams.

Many hikers and budding geologists visit Clearwater

Lake Provincial Park to hike the Caves Self-Guiding Trail. "The Caves" are deep crevices that were formed when rock masses separated from the shoreline cliffs, leaving cave-like spaces and vertical fractures between layers of dolomite bedrock. Park staff have built stairways and viewing platforms along the designated trail, and they're quick to warn you to stay on the path, both for your own safety and to protect the sensitive plant life in the area. Wildlife, such as black bears, squirrels and weasels, use the cave-like spaces for shelter.

In addition to fishing, other diversions include swimming, boating, hiking and camping. In the winter, park staff maintain a day-use area east of Pioneer Bay for visitors to enjoy cross-country skiing, skating and tobogganing.

Clearwater Lake is a few kilometres south of another interesting geological feature: the Cusp of The Pas Moraine, a crescent-like escarpment formed during the last ice age. The Pas Moraine, which is 16 kilometres wide, rises 60 metres above the surrounding terrain, making it one of the most prominent glacial formations in central Manitoba.

↑ The crystalline Clearwater Lake takes up almost half of the 593-square-kilometre park.

← The clear quality of the lake's water is due to the fact that it's spring fed and doesn't contain the sediment that is typically carried into river-fed lakes.

↓ "The Caves" are deep crevices that were formed when rock masses separated from the shoreline cliffs.

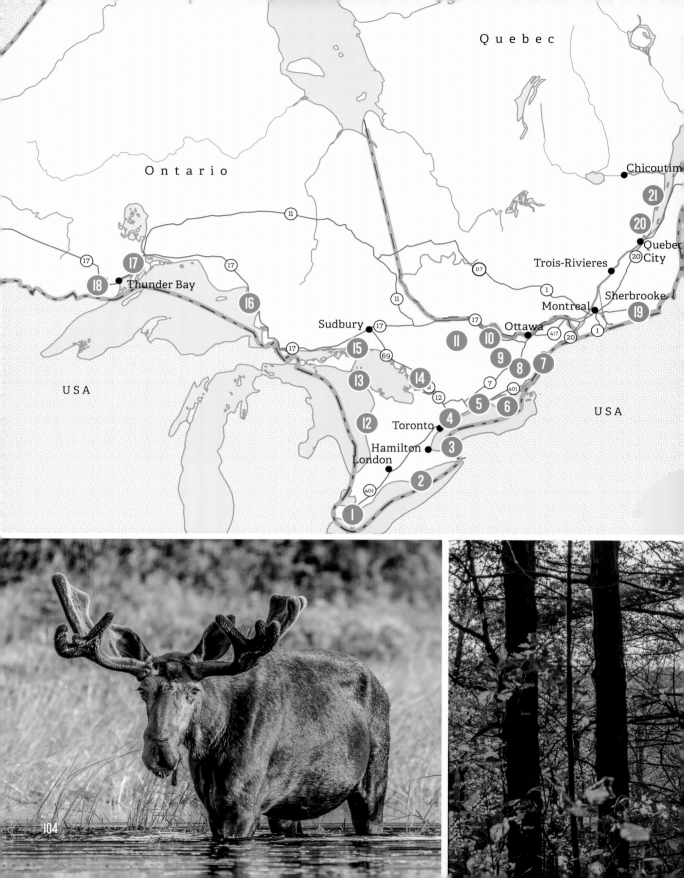

25

24

23

22

Iles

Prince
Edward
Island

New Brunswick

Nova
Scotia

*Atlantic
Ocean*

# Central Canada

## Ontario

## Quebec

# Point Pelee National Park

by Chris Earley

**Visitors will find North America's best inland bird migration site at the southernmost tip of mainland Canada**

## What Makes This Hot Spot Hot?

- Birders from all over the world come here to see the spring migration.
- Point Pelee has been dubbed the "Warbler capital of North America": The record number of warbler species seen by an individual birder in one day is 34.
- Walk to the tip and become the southernmost mainland person in Canada.

**Address:** 1118 Point Pelee Dr, Leamington, ON
**GPS:** 41.96277; −82.51844
**Tel.:** (519) 322-2365
**Website:** www.pc.gc.ca/en /pn-np/on/pelee/index

**Open year-round**

♿ (Check ahead)

↗ **The sweet-singing American redstart breeds at Point Pelee. Hopping from branch to branch, this warbler uses its dramatic colour to startle its insect prey into the open.**

→ **Watch for turtles and fish from the marsh boardwalk.**

If you want to see birds during spring migration, this is the spot. Vireos, flycatchers, orioles, sparrows, warblers — they're all here. Mid-May is Point Pelee's peak time for both birds and birders, and while it can be busy, the density of people also makes it a great spot for beginners to get help. Most birders are only too willing to fill in newbies on the habits of that difficult vireo sitting overhead or to identify the strange song coming from the shrubs.

Point Pelee is a great spring migration spot largely because of its long southern reach into Lake Erie. Most small birds are nocturnal migrants and may fly hundreds of kilometres in one night. If they're still over the lake once morning comes, they have no choice but to continue flying until they reach land. Point Pelee might be the first spot they see, which funnels many birds into the park's beach, forest, savannah, swamp and marsh habitats.

But Point Pelee isn't only about birds. You may find an endangered eastern fox snake sunning itself on the side of a trail, a brilliant yellow hairy puccoon in full bloom near the beach or a juniper hairstreak butterfly sitting on an eastern red cedar. And don't miss the marsh boardwalk. It's an excellent place to watch for turtles, and a short walk might turn up snapping, northern map, painted or Blanding's turtles taking a break in the sun. You may also see some of the marsh's fish life as you gaze into the water — perhaps a long-time park denizen such as the spotted gar, a primitive ray-finned fish whose family has made North America home for the past 100 million years.

# Long Point Provincial Park

by Chris Earley

*Morning bird banding, a picnic lunch on the beach, an afternoon visit to the marsh and an evening search for an endangered toad — there's much to discover all day*

## What Makes This Hot Spot Hot?

- Four hundred species of birds have been recorded in the Long Point area.
- There's an expansive marsh that attracts huge flocks of migrating waterfowl.
- Visitors can explore the area on foot, by bicycle, by canoe or by boat.

**Address:** 350 Erie Blvd, Port Rowan, ON
**GPS:** 42.58166; −80.39517
**Tel.:** (519) 586-2133
**Websites:** www.ontarioparks .com/park/longpoint and www.birdscanada .org/longpoint

**Open mid-May to mid-October**

&#9855; (Check ahead)

↗ **A sand-covered Fowler's toad might show itself to beachcombers during a nighttime stroll at Long Point.**

A UNESCO World Biosphere Reserve, Long Point is a roughly 40-kilometre-long sand spit that juts out into Lake Erie from the lake's northern shore. One of the best places in Canada to watch birds, Long Point is home to the Long Point National Wildlife Area, Long Point Provincial Park and the Long Point Bird Observatory. An important migration site, the park and the surrounding region also provide vital nesting areas for over 175 species of birds.

This spot is home to a considerable number of species at risk, including the Fowler's toad. This endangered amphibian is in decline across Ontario, and Long Point is one of only three places where it still survives. Habitat degradation, vehicle use on beaches and pesticides are all implicated in its falling numbers. An evening hike along the over 1.5 kilometres

of sandy beach of Long Point Provincial Park may allow you to find and watch one of these rare amphibians, but be sure to not disturb it.

Just outside the provincial park entrance is the Old Cut Research Station. This is part of the Long Point Bird Observatory, the oldest observatory of its kind in the western hemisphere. A morning visit to Old Cut during the spring (April to June) or fall (August to November) allows you to see firsthand how researchers catch and band birds. By re-catching birds that have already been previously banded, researchers gain a much more sophisticated understanding of the migration routes, physiological changes and population fluctuations of our birds. In 2014, Long Point Bird Observatory banded 26,683 birds from 166 species. Since it opened in 1960, it has banded 275 different bird species and almost one million individual birds.

↑ Banding little-known species, such as the Connecticut warbler, can reveal much to researchers.

↖ An aerial view of Long Point, a 40-kilometre sand spit that juts into Lake Erie.

# Niagara River

by Chris Earley

### *Winter birders will have fun gulling along the Niagara Gorge*

## What Makes This Hot Spot Hot?

- The Niagara corridor is the first site in North America to achieve recognition as a Globally Significant Important Bird Area.
- In November and December, the variety of gulls at Niagara is greater than anywhere else on Earth.
- There are amazing views of the gorge walls, the rushing river and the three waterfalls that make up Niagara Falls.

**Address:** Niagara Pkwy between Niagara-on-the-Lake and Niagara Falls, ON
**GPS:** 43.25641; −79.06321
**Tel.:** (877) 642-7275
**Website:** www.niagaraparks.com

**Open year-round**

&#x1F4F7; &#x1F6B6;

&#x267F; (Check ahead)

Even the most resistant naturalist eventually falls under the spell of gull identification, and one of the best places on the planet to watch them turns out to be the Niagara River in November and December. Fourteen gull species have been seen here in one day, which is a world record. And since this seemingly blah time of year is sandwiched between the beautiful fall colours of October and the snowy blankets of January, birders often flock to the river to see what they can find.

Starting at the mouth of the river in Niagara-on-the-Lake, ease into identification by looking for the three most common species of gulls at this time: the herring gull, ring-billed gull and Bonaparte's gull. This is a great place to watch for other birds, too, such as red-throated loons, long-tailed ducks and horned grebes.

Travelling up the river by car, there are many stops to make. At Queenston, scan the flocks of gulls for a little gull (the world's smallest gull is the size of a mourning dove) or a great black-backed gull (the world's largest gull, which is the size of a turkey vulture). The overlook at Adam Beck Power Dam is a wonderful place from which to look down at flying gulls, which makes the identification of Arctic species such as the glaucous gull or Iceland gull much easier.

At Niagara Falls, peer through the mist and see if you can find usually oceanic species, such as black-legged

↗ **An immature black-legged kittiwake drops in on Niagara.**

kittiwakes or Sabine's gulls. Above the falls, scan through resting gulls to look for a lesser black-backed gull or Thayer's gull. Carefully check the rocks here for a purple sandpiper, and take a look at all the different duck species as well. All along your river-edge travels, watch for southern Ontario specialty birds such as the black vulture, tufted titmouse, Carolina wren and northern mockingbird. And remember, Niagara is a perfect place to shake away those November birder blahs.

↑ **Where's Waldo? Can you find the one lesser black-backed gull in this resting flock?**

# Rouge National Urban Park

by Tracy C. Read

**For city dwellers, this park is the natural wonderland of a lifetime**

## What Makes This Hot Spot Hot?

- This huge park is within driving distance of one-fifth of Canada's population.
- The Rouge is home to an abundance of species of plants and animals, both familiar and uncommon.
- It is the first national park to be established in an urban area.

**Address:** 1749 Meadowvale Rd, Scarborough, ON
**GPS:** 43.81879; –79.17086
**Tel.:** (416) 264-2020
**Website:** www.pc.gc.ca /en/pn-np/on/rouge/index

**Open year-round; trails are not maintained in winter**

♿ (Check ahead)

↗ **Autumn colour in Canada's first national urban park.**

In a collection that celebrates Canada's nature hot spots, it would be impossible to ignore the Rouge. In reality, there are countless hot spots in this vast urban park, which is a sprawling 79 square kilometres that stretches from the Oak Ridges Moraine to Lake Ontario, with the Rouge River system as its centrepiece.

Situated near 20 per cent of Canada's population, the Rouge National Urban Park is explicitly regarded as an opportunity for city-dwelling Canadians to connect with the country's natural heritage. The Rouge has been protected by decades of dedicated local stewardship, but with federal involvement came collaborative aquatic habitat enhancement, wetland restoration, native plantings and the protection of threatened species, among other initiatives.

The Rouge is a crazy quilt of landscapes, from rivers and creeks, geological outcrops, hoodoos and gullies, drumlins and flutes to high-level terraces, marshes, woodlands and meadows, right down to the sandy spit where the Rouge River flows into Lake Ontario. The sheer variety of habitats leads naturally to biodiversity. Rouge Park has that in abundance, with more than 1,000 plant species and over 380 species of birds, fish, mammals,

reptiles and amphibians, many of which are nationally and regionally rare.

Via a network of trails, visitors can hike through old-growth forest and woodlands as red squirrels race up and down the trees, listen to a bobolink or a yellow warbler in a quiet, leafy glen or view a red-tailed hawk surveying the landscape from on high. In the early morning and early evening, the sounds of spring peepers and grey tree frogs fill the air, and in spring and summer, the buzzing of insects reverberates all around. Lookouts offer panoramic views of the bluffs and river valleys.

For residents of the Greater Toronto Area, it's a backyard wonderland that could take a lifetime to explore.

↑ **Canada geese take flight in the fall.**

↖ **A wetland vista in the Rouge.**

# Presqu'ile Provincial Park

by Kyle Horner

*Jutting into Lake Ontario, this provincial park offers a lot of diversity in a small package*

## What Makes This Hot Spot Hot?

- Its unusual geography and geology create an exceptional diversity of habitats.
- It boasts some of the best migration birding on the shore of Lake Ontario.
- The park offers excellent visitor services and education programs, and it is conveniently located for visitors.

**Address:** 328 Presqu'ile Pkwy, Brighton, ON
**GPS:** 44.0098; –77.74203
**Tel.:** (613) 475-4324
**Website:** www.ontarioparks .com/park/presquile

**Open year-round for day use; camping from May 1 to mid-October**

♿ (Check ahead)

↗ A monarch touches down at the "almost island" that is Presqu'ile.

Located roughly halfway between the Greater Toronto Area and Kingston, this provincial park is aptly named after the French word for "almost island." Presqu'ile is what is known as a tombolo — a gradual accretion of sand that has created a connecting spit between a limestone island and the mainland. This "almost island" projects into the smallest of the Great Lakes, and its unusual geography and geology has resulted in the park harbouring an interesting inventory of habitats.

The spit's west-facing side is exposed to the lake's wind and waves. The constant pushing action has resulted in an expansive beach, popular with swimmers, picnickers and windsurfers. The beach is framed by some of Lake Ontario's best dune habitat, which supports an incredibly diverse plant community. By contrast, the sheltered east-facing side is home to the largest protected marsh on the northern shore of the lake, which provides habitat for abundant waterfowl, fish

↑ **A boardwalk snakes through the park's grassy wetland.**

and other wildlife. The "island" portion of the park is made up of mixed forests and meadows and hosts yet another community of species.

While Presqu'ile teems with life in all seasons, its spring and fall bird migrations are exceptional, and that's largely due to its varied habitats. The forests and meadows attract songbirds of every colour, while waterfowl settle in the marsh and shorebirds forage on the beach. Over 330 bird species have been recorded here, making it one of Ontario's premier migration birding locations. In autumn, monarch butterflies also rest here in large numbers before setting off across the lake.

Presqu'ile offers both camping and day-use opportunities and is equally rewarding as a day on the beach or a hike in the forest. Two visitor centres are open throughout the summer season, and education programs and guided hikes are offered daily. With so much to see, you're sure to be planning your next visit before you leave.

# Sandbanks Provincial Park

by Tracy C. Read

*There is much, much more to this park than fun in the sun*

## What Makes This Hot Spot Hot?

- Sandbanks is the site of the world's largest freshwater bay mouth sand barrier dune formation.
- This sandy projection into Lake Ontario makes Sandbanks a bird-migration mecca in spring and fall.
- Walking trails allow visitors to fully experience the park's dune and wetland habitats.

**Address:** 3004 County Rd 12, RR 1, Picton, ON
**GPS:** 43.90702; −77.23922
**Tel.:** (613) 393-3319
**Website:** www.ontarioparks .com/park/sandbanks

**Open year-round; camping from May 1 to mid-October**

**Note that springtime flooding and high water levels may affect access to the park's trails, beaches and campgrounds. Please check local conditions before planning a visit.**

&#9855; (Check ahead)

One of the most popular provincial parks in Ontario, Sandbanks is located on Prince Edward County's southwestern shore. Beloved for its long stretches of stunning sand beaches and the pounding Lake Ontario surf, the park hosts large numbers of visitors who come every summer to camp, swim and bask in the sun.

Yet Sandbanks is far more than a sunny playground. Some 10,000 years ago, the wild westerly winds of Lake Ontario began to relentlessly push sand into the nooks and crannies of this headland. The vast bay mouth sand barrier that eventually formed here is a dynamic, ever-changing and fragile ecosystem and is the largest freshwater sandbar and dune system in the world.

When the 1,600-hectare provincial park was first conceived in the early 1970s, it was designed to link two dune systems with the farmland and wooded area that separated them. As a result, the park protects a range of habitats that host uncommon

flora and fauna, and naturalists are drawn to the park in great numbers. Sandbanks is particularly valued as a birding destination during the spring and fall migrations, and more than 240 species have been observed here, including the red-headed woodpecker, pileated woodpecker, Baltimore oriole and ruby-crowned kinglet.

The park takes its role in educating the public about the value of this distinctive place seriously. In addition to daily interpretive programming during the summer, there is a 2.5-kilometre loop trail through the fragile dune and wetland habitat. Regionally rare bird species, including the marsh wren, make their home in the park. Here, too, grow distinctive dune species of flora, such as bluet, butterfly weed and sand surge. Cyclists and hikers can take a trail through old farm pastures and hardwood lots, while a 12-stop interpretive trail follows the shores of the Outlet River and features two lookouts with scenic views of the marsh.

↰↑ **Vegetation creeps into the park's sand dune system, while its vast sandy beaches draw sun lovers from near and far.**

# Thousand Islands

by Tracy C. Read

**The rewards of exploring this not-so-lazy river are thousandfold**

## What Makes This Hot Spot Hot?

- Home to Thousand Islands National Park, the area has dozens of campsites as well as oTENTik camping.
- Here, north meets south, and with the moderating effects of Lake Ontario, an abundance of species coexist.
- For the paddle-phobic, there are mainland trails near Mallorytown.

**Address:** 1121 Thousand Islands Pkwy, Mallorytown, ON
**GPS:** 44.45396; −75.85905
**Tel.:** (613) 923-5261;
(888) 773-8888
**Website:** www.pc.gc.ca /en/pn-np/on/1000/index

**Open May to October**

**Note that springtime flooding and high water levels may affect access to the park's trails, docks, islands and campgrounds. Please check local conditions before planning a visit.**

&#9855; (Check ahead)

↗ **An idyllic glimpse of sky, water, trees and land in the Thousand Islands.**

One of Ontario's most famous summer playgrounds, the Thousand Islands are an archipelago that spans the Canada–U.S. border along the St. Lawrence River. On the Canadian side, they are scattered over some 80 kilometres, from the outlet of Lake Ontario, near Kingston, to Brockville. These islands and outcroppings are part of the Frontenac Arch, a narrow granite remnant that links the Canadian Shield in the north to the Adirondack Mountains in the south. They've been scrubbed, scoured and shaped by glaciers, leaving a legacy of windswept trees, bluffs, granite cliffs, beaches, potholes and wide-ranging rock formations.

The region's Indigenous Peoples also regarded the river and islands as a place of seasonal bounty, travelling here to fish, hunt and trade rather than settling permanently. But despite the annual invasion of cottagers and boaters, the islands remain a remarkable setting in which to experience one of the province's most varied and beautiful landscapes.

Exploring the area by canoe or kayak affords the best opportunities to appreciate the richly diverse ecosystems. As you paddle alongside granite cliffs, you might spot petroglyphs and pictographs inscribed by Indigenous Peoples thousands of years ago. Northern and southern forest types and their residents live side by side, sometimes on the same island. Small mammals and birds, such as sparrows, orioles, wrens, warblers and owls, dwell in the mixed forest, while ring-billed and herring

gulls nest on small islets and fish-hunting ospreys circle overhead. In the river-edge wetlands, watch for turtles, beavers and muskrats as well as ducks, geese, herons and an occasional sighting of the least bittern.

The snorkelling is superb (but be wary of the currents), and the clear water gives naturalists a chance to observe the hardest-to- observe of the vertebrates: fish. In some areas, the river offers long vistas, which make sky watching a lazy way to link with nature. Learn your cloud formations, and keep an eye out for such day-sky phenomena as sun dogs, sun pillars and rainbows.

⬆ A trio of Toronto Blue Jays fans takes a closer look at a beautiful pumpkinseed sunfish that has been temporarily scooped into an aquarium.

⬉ An aerial view illustrates why a boat is the best way to explore the islands.

# Frontenac Provincial Park

by Tracy C. Read

**_Geological eras clash, and paddlers, hikers and campers savour an ecological sweet spot in this wilderness playground_**

## What Makes This Hot Spot Hot?

- This park boasts a rich diversity of plant, bird, mammal, snake, butterfly and dragonfly species.
- For those who want to rent canoes and other gear, Frontenac Outfitters is located just outside the park gates.
- Half an hour north of Kingston, Frontenac Park is Canadian Shield country at its best — and much more.

**Address:** 6700 Salmon Lake Rd, Sydenham, ON
**GPS:** 44.50767; −76.55316
**Tel.:** (613) 376-3489
**Website:** www.frontenacpark.ca

**Open year-round**

↗ **A great blue heron wades through a Frontenac marsh in full bloom.**

F our seasons of the year, eastern Ontarians are fiercely loyal to Frontenac Provincial Park, with good reason. This park has something for every outdoor lover. A half-hour drive north of Kingston, Frontenac sits on the southernmost edge of the Canadian Shield, in an area known as the Frontenac Arch. At the confluence of five forest regions, the Arch links the boreal forest of the Canadian Shield in the north to the forests of the Adirondack and Appalachian Mountains to the south. The landform is a dramatic interruption of the otherwise flat countryside of southern Ontario. And what an interruption: A remarkable melding of north and south, it's a landscape of forests and lakes, wetlands and rugged cliffs formed from exposed Precambrian rock.

Frontenac embraces 5,355 hectares of this wild area. Dotted with 22 lakes and bordered by an additional six, the park draws paddlers eager to experience a range of canoe routes — some explore the classic deep, clear, cold, low-vegetation lakes of the Shield, while others head to more southerly examples of

warm, shallow, weedy bodies of water. Hikers, too, enjoy a surfeit of choice, with more than 100 kilometres of interconnected trails, while for geology fans, the park represents a rich banquet. During the last ice age, glacial activity carved out a system of alternating ridges and valleys in this region, and all across the park is evidence of the unmistakable impact of kilometre-thick continental ice sheets scraping away bedrock and soil and polishing and radically resculpting billion-year-old Precambrian rocks.

A transition zone between the ranges for northern and southern plants, Frontenac nurtures some 700 species — almost half of the plant life found in Ontario. An estimated 50 locally important sites support rare species of ferns, sedges, mosses and orchids. Roughly 25 species of mammals make the park their home, from the tiny, plentiful voles and shrews to the white-tailed deer, black bear and moose. In the woodland, wetlands and along lakeshores, more than 170 bird species, including the rarely seen red-shouldered hawk, can be found.

↑ Sun-warmed rock on the edge of Birch Lake.

↖ A patch of blue sky lingers during sunset on Kingsford Lake, at the park's northwest border.

# Bon Echo Provincial Park

by Kyle Horner

*French for "good echo," Bon Echo was named for the effects of its most prominent feature: the towering and formidable Mazinaw Rock*

## What Makes This Hot Spot Hot?

- Bon Echo features one of Canada's best Indigenous pictograph sites.
- Abundant wildlife, including rare species that take advantage of cliff habitats, make the park their home.
- There are plenty of hiking, paddling, wildlife viewing and photo opportunities.

**Address:** 16151 Hwy 41, Cloyne, ON
**GPS:** 44.8973; −77.20978
**Tel.:** (613) 336-2228
**Website:** www.ontarioparks.com/park/bonecho

**Open mid-May to mid-October**

&#9855; (Check ahead)

Meet Ontario's only lizard: the five-lined skink.

At 100 metres tall and 1.5 kilometres long, Mazinaw Rock dominates the landscape of Bon Echo Provincial Park. Formed by volcanic activity and glaciation, the rock plunges to a depth of 145 metres in Mazinaw Lake. This geological colossus has long captured the attention of campers, paddlers and daring climbers, and it is why the area was first established as a tourist destination in the late 1800s. Long before European settlement, though, Mazinaw was an important place for the area's Indigenous Peoples.

To view one of the largest rock art sites in Canada, rent a canoe or take an interpretive tour on the park's boat, a 26-passenger cruise vessel named *The Wanderer*. Mazinaw Rock is adorned with more than 260 Indigenous pictographs, believed to have been painted by the Algonquin People. The word Mazinaw itself comes from the Algonquin language, meaning, roughly, "painted rock." Rendered in red ochre, the paintings depict animals, humans, geographic forms and abstract symbols. Their age has not been established.

**↑ Cliffs rise majestically from Bon Echo's Mazinaw Lake.**

Humans are not the only creatures drawn to Mazinaw Rock — interesting wildlife species also take advantage of the unique landform. Peregrine falcons nest here and can be seen circling overhead or plummeting to the water as they hunt for an unsuspecting duck or gull. Ontario's only lizard — the five-lined skink — also lives here, sheltered among the moss and broken rocks that litter the exposed Canadian Shield. An abundance of other wildlife calls the park home, and the keen observer will not be disappointed.

Bon Echo Provincial Park is perfect for a day visit but also provides camping facilities, from fully serviced to backcountry. Hiking trails range from 1 to 17 kilometres, including the spectacular Cliff Top Trail, which provides stunning views of the park. Paddling may be the best way to see Bon Echo, however, and it allows visitors to share perspective with the Indigenous Peoples and Europeans who came before.

# Bonnechere Caves

by Tracy C. Read

*Spelunkers can step into a time machine on the shores of the Bonnechere River*

## What Makes This Hot Spot Hot?

- The Bonnechere Caves are one of North America's best examples of a solution cave — created when acidic groundwater dissolves the stone.
- The scalloped walls are a veritable library of ancient marine-life fossils.
- The caves are situated near one of the prettiest waterfalls in the area.

**Address:** 1247 Fourth Chute Rd, Eganville, ON
**GPS:** 45.50469; −77.00928
**Tel.:** (613) 628-2283
**Website:** www.bonnecherecaves.com

**Open daily from May long weekend through September 30; open weekends until Thanksgiving**

Long before the Bonnechere Caves existed, much of North America, including what is now the Ottawa Valley, was bathed in the waters of a warm, tropical sea. Some 450 million years ago, the Ordovician period was characterized by the intense diversification of marine animals — fish and other creatures with backbones were not quite on the evolutionary horizon, but the sea teemed with invertebrate life. The period ended with a mass extinction, but thanks to the blankets of sediment the sea had deposited over time, some of these marine animals were perfectly preserved as fossils.

Let's speed through the rough ride the continent endured before the last ice age, about 10,000 years ago. As glaciers melted and retreated

↙→ **Boardwalks lead visitors through a sculpted interior created over thousands of years by acidic groundwaters.**

from the limestone that underlies the Ottawa Valley, the landscape as we know it today — lakes, rivers and rolling hills — eventually took shape. The carbonic acid present in moving groundwater can dissolve bedrock over time, and as water flowed along the course of what is now the Bonnechere River, it worked its magic on the limestone riverbed. After thousands of years, the caves emerged — not carved away by the brutal action of grinding glaciers but, instead, "melted" away by the acidic groundwater.

The privately managed Bonnechere Caves are a dark, damp habitat, perhaps made even more mysterious for that. As we gaze upon the dramatically sculpted walls, where the fossils of generations of ancient sea creatures have been captured in perpetuity, it's hard not to be entranced by what time has fashioned. Once you've explored the caves, come out into the sunlit present and visit the Fourth Chute, a beautiful cascading waterfall on the Bonnechere River.

# Algonquin Provincial Park

by Debbie Olsen

*More than 2,400 lakes and 1,200 kilometres of rivers, creeks and streams can be found in Canada's oldest provincial park*

## What Makes This Hot Spot Hot?

- The park's pristine lakes and rivers are a paddling paradise.
- There is an incredible diversity of plant and animal species.
- Algonquin's stunning scenery has inspired artists like Tom Thomson and members of the Group of Seven.

**Address**: Hwy 60 at km 43, Whitney, ON
**GPS**: 45.583922; −78.359455
**Tel.**: (705) 633-5572
**Websites**: www.algonquinpark .on.ca and www.ontarioparks .com/park/algonquin

**Open year-round**

&#9855; (Check ahead)

Established in 1893, Algonquin Provincial Park was Canada's first provincial park. It pioneered visitor interpretation programs and park management practices that have been used in other parks across the country. In 1992 the park was named a National Historic Site of Canada, recognizing its pioneering efforts, its historic infrastructure and its role inspiring artists whose works have given Canadians a greater sense of their country. Canada's famous Group of Seven artists considered calling themselves the "Algonquin School" because of their strong connection to the park.

## Wildlife

Algonquin is one of the best places in North America to see moose. The park encompasses a transition zone between northern coniferous forests and southern deciduous forests. The wide variety of ecosystems support diverse flora and fauna and make the park an important site for wildlife research. Moose, black bears, white-tailed

deer, beavers, red foxes and Algonquin wolves are a few of the mammals that reside here.

The meeting of two forests also results in a diverse array of birdlife. Some 285 species of birds have been seen in the park. Canada jays, spruce grouse, boreal chickadees and black-backed woodpeckers are four boreal species popular with birders year-round. A wide variety of migratory birds can also be seen, including many different species of warblers, white-throated sparrows, red-eyed vireos, barred owls and common loons. The Friends of Algonquin Park produce a species checklist and a book with detailed information on the birds of Algonquin. The park posts a winter birding report on its website, which has an up-to-date list of the latest bird sightings, and www.ebird.ca also posts recent checklists.

## Canoeing and Canoe Camping

Algonquin is a paddler's paradise, with 2,000 kilometres of canoe routes and portages. Most regions of the vast interior wilderness can only be reached by canoe, and this is why canoe camping is such a popular activity here. The Friends of Algonquin Park produces an official back-country canoe tripping map that is continually updated by park staff to reflect current conditions. You can browse online and purchase a full-sized printed copy for a small fee. The map shows canoe routes, campsites, portages,

↑ Algonquin Park is famous for its stunning fall colours, which can be enjoyed by land and water.

← Moose are a common sight in Algonquin Park, but be sure to keep a safe distance from these majestic giants.

environmental factors affect the timing of the change in leaf colours, so it can vary slightly from year to year. The sugar maple and red maple trees usually reach their peak red fall colours the last week of September or the first week of October. Aspen, larch and red oak usually peak shortly afterward. Check the online Ontario Parks Fall Colour Report for the latest foliage updates.

## Interpretive Walking Trails

There are 15 themed interpretive walking trails along the Highway 60 corridor, and each one has a published guide to help you discover the trail's unique features. Among the many trails are a few standouts, like Bat Lake Trail. The highlight of this 5.8-kilometre loop is a naturally acidic fishless lake that is a paradise for budding entomologists. The trail passes through a beautiful hemlock stand as well as boggy wetlands, and it's common to see many species of dragonflies and damselflies, especially in early July.

The 10.8-kilometre Mizzy Lake Trail is a wildlife watcher's paradise. This relatively flat trail visits nine ponds and small lakes, but you don't need to hike the entire trail to see wildlife. The most popular section is between Wolf Howl Pond and West Rose Lake, and you can drive to the

lakes, access points and helpful tips on backcountry trip planning.

## Fall Foliage

Early autumn is one of the prettiest seasons in Algonquin Park, and many people visit to see the stunning fall foliage. The park is home to 34 native species of trees, including substantial stands of mature sugar maple, hemlock and yellow birch. Some of the oldest trees are estimated to be up to 610 years old. A variety of access point. Go early in the morning and look for birds and other wildlife, such as moose, beavers, otters and turtles.

The Spruce Bog Boardwalk is a 1.5-kilometre wheelchair-accessible boardwalk that provides easy access to a fascinating habitat that is normally very difficult to get to — two northern spruce bogs. A copy of the park's trail guide will help you identify the abundant bog-adapted plants you see along this trail. Watch for spruce grouse, the most sought-after wildlife sighting in this area of the park.

↑ The alligator boat is an amphibious vessel that was used for the forestry industry across Canada.

← The Spruce Bog Boardwalk is a chance to look at one of nature's most interesting habitats.

↙ The spruce grouse is known to be very tame around humans, which makes them a great bird to observe.

## Park Facilities

To explore the educational interactive displays, exhibits and art of Algonquin Provincial Park, you'll want to visit its outstanding facilities. The Algonquin Visitor Centre is located at kilometre 43 of Highway 60. This year-round centre is the place to go to get park info and permits. It houses exhibits on the park's natural and human history, a restaurant, a bookstore and a theatre that screens a film about the park. Be sure to take in the view from the observation deck.

Algonquin has long been a source of inspiration for artists, and the Algonquin Art Centre showcases works from established and up-and-coming Canadian wilderness and wildlife artists. There's also an artist-in-residence program, exhibitions and unique programming. The art gallery is located at kilometre 20 of Highway 60.

Lastly, the Algonquin Logging Museum tells the long history of logging within the park, from its earliest days to the present. Though logging in Algonquin is controversial, the museum is meant to showcase sustainable methods of modern forestry management. There's a video presentation, a bookstore and a 1.5-kilometre interpretive trail with a re-created camboose camp and a steam-powered "alligator" boat as the main attractions. Take a look and decide for yourself if this activity is still appropriate in Canada's oldest provincial park. The museum is located at kilometre 54.5 of Highway 60.

# MacGregor Point Provincial Park

by Kyle Horner

***Located on one of the most beautiful sections of the Lake Huron shoreline, MacGregor Point hosts an impressive bird migration and year-round wildlife***

## What Makes This Hot Spot Hot?

- This is a pristine piece of Lake Huron shoreline, with a diversity of inland forests and waterways.
- There is excellent migration birding and an annual spring birding festival.
- The visitor centre, friendly staff and excellent educational programming are all part of MacGregor Point's magic.

**Address:** 1593 Bruce Rd 33, RR 1, Port Elgin, ON
**GPS:** 44.41391; −81.45526
**Tel.:** (519) 389-9056
**Websites:** www.ontarioparks .com/park/macgregorpoint and www.friendsofmacgregor.org

**Open year-round**

&#9855; (Check ahead)

With windswept dunes and rocky beaches, the Lake Huron shoreline is like no other place in Ontario. MacGregor Point Provincial Park encompasses a 7-kilometre stretch of this unique habitat, and trails and boardwalks allow the visitor to experience it first-hand. Farther inland, the park comprises mixed forests punctuated by maple swamps, cattail marshes, bogs, fens and ponds. These varied waterways support a great diversity of wildlife.

Walking the coastal dunes often provides great viewing opportunities for a variety of bird life, including gulls, terns, shorebirds and osprey. Northern water snakes live here, too, hiding among the grasses and heading out to the lake to fish. On calmer days, dragonflies and butterflies forage along the dunes as well, and hardy wildflowers brave the challenging environment in the spring and summer. The park's bogs support a community of

↑ **A spotted turtle pokes its head out from a grassy shoreline.**

← **A dragonfly is trapped by the carnivorous spatulate-leaved sundew.**

carnivorous plants, including pitcher plants and the diminutive sundews. Endangered spotted turtles have been seen, and the ponds are home to a wide variety of ducks and herons.

For many naturalists, MacGregor's biggest draw is its spectacular population of migratory birds. It is a fruitful stopover for birds travelling up the shore of the lake, and on a given day in the spring, the trees may be filled with colourful warblers, vireos, tanagers and orioles. The Friends of MacGregor Point Provincial Park host the annual Huron Fringe Birding Festival here, which features guided bird hikes, workshops and guest speakers.

Whether for camping or a day visit, MacGregor Point exposes visitors to an ecosystem seen almost nowhere else in Ontario. A quick stop at the visitor centre, with its informative exhibits and friendly staff, will get you started in your exploration. For those wanting a more thorough introduction, the park offers many excellent education programs throughout the summer season.

↑ **A boardwalk trail through the mixed forest at MacGregor Point Provincial Park.**

# Bruce Peninsula National Park

by Chris Earley

*Visitors will tour of some of Ontario's most breathtaking vistas*

## What Makes This Hot Spot Hot?

- It features a continuous cliff with forest and lake views.
- These ancient cedars have been around since the 1300s.
- Hike the famous Bruce Trail, which ends in beautiful Tobermory.

**Address:** 469 Cyprus Lake Rd, Tobermory, ON
**GPS:** 45.22881; −81.52325
**Tel.:** (519) 596-2233
**Website:** www.pc.gc.ca/en /pn-np/on/bruce/index

**Open year-round**

🔭 (Check ahead)

↗ **Cedars eke out a living in the crevices and fissures of escarpment rock.**

The Niagara Escarpment is essentially the edge of a giant basin whose centre is in the middle of the state of Michigan. Travelling north from Niagara to the eastern side of the Bruce Peninsula, the escarpment continues, though broken with watery gaps, to Manitoulin Island. From there, it runs all the way to Wisconsin's Door Peninsula, which is the western side of the Michigan Basin.

The escarpment in the Bruce Peninsula National Park is nothing short of breathtaking, and a number of park trails allow you to explore both the top and the bottom of the cliff faces. A popular destination is the Grotto, where it's possible to climb down into a partially submerged cave. Halfway Log Dump, Cave Point, Overhanging Point and Indian Head Cove are other especially appealing spots to visit.

While you may be wowed by the views alone, the trees

↑ The signature turquoise waters off the Bruce Peninsula.

growing out from the sides of the cliffs will surely inspire a different sense of awe. Despite their diminutive size, some of the northern white cedars here are hundreds of years old: The oldest known specimen in the park is over 850 years old. These cedars grow very slowly due to the harsh conditions and are part of a cliff eco-system that includes lichens, ferns and mosses.

Wildlife and wildflower viewing in the park can easily keep a naturalist busy from early morning to nightfall. The shape of the peninsula funnels spring migratory birds flying northbound through the park's forests, and waterfowl can be found along the shore-lines. The park has dozens of species each of orchids and ferns as well as many other herbaceous plants waiting to be identified. A winter visit reveals the tracks of coyotes, foxes, fishers, snowshoe hares and porcupines.

# Thirty Thousand Islands

by Chris Earley

***This scenic stretch of Georgian Bay is home to the world's largest freshwater archipelago***

## What Makes This Hot Spot Hot?

- There are impressive Canadian Shield landscapes at the water's edge.
- Georgian Bay's clear water is perfect for under-the-surface wildlife watching.
- Watch out for rare reptiles and plant life on your hikes.

**Address**: Trans-Canada Hwy (Hwy 400) between Port Severn and French River, ON
**GPS**: 44.89049; −79.75612
**Tel.**: (800) 668-2746
**Websites**: www.ontarioparks .com, www.pc.gc.ca/en/pn-np /on/georg/index and www.gblt.org

**Contact individual parks for information about seasonal closures**

> The smooth green snake is arguably Ontario's prettiest snake species.

The eastern shoreline of Georgian Bay is one of Ontario's most dramatic landscapes. Windswept, rugged and wild, it is dotted with tens of thousands of islands collectively known as the Thirty Thousand Islands. It's the world's largest freshwater archipelago, and while private cottages are plentiful, there are many government-run parks that the public is welcome to enjoy and explore — Killbear, Awenda and Sturgeon Bay Provincial Parks and Georgian Bay Islands National Park among them.

In addition, the Georgian Bay Land Trust and the Nature Conservancy of Canada oversee several properties that allow visitors as well. This mixture of accessible and non-accessible areas creates the best of both worlds: Beautiful places for the naturalist to visit and reservoirs of wildlife habitat to protect nature from human harm.

The ideal — and sometimes only — way to explore the Thirty Thousand Islands is by watercraft. Kayaking is the preferred means for many reasons: It offers access to very

↑ **This is just one of the spectacular Thirty Thousand Islands.**

shallow water, easy manoeuvrability and a quiet approach for wildlife watching. While floating around in a kayak, you might see a muskrat or northern map turtle swim underneath you or a northern pike slowly turn its body before torpedoing forward to grab a minnow. Along the shorelines, watch for the praying mantis-like water scorpions seizing a smaller aquatic insect or a giant water bug father carrying his mate's eggs on his back.

While hiking along gorgeous granite formations, look out for Ontario's only lizard species, the endangered five-lined skink. Young individuals stand out with their brilliant blue tails, while the older generations are duller overall. Another colourful reptile found here is the smooth green snake, which slithers along looking very much like a live lime-green shoelace. Watch for brilliant wildflowers, too, such as Kalm's lobelia and the cardinal flower. And don't forget to finish up by appreciating the day's last colours as the shimmering sun sets across the bay.

# Killarney Provincial Park

by Chris Earley

*This storied provincial park is a paddling naturalist's dream destination*

## What Makes This Hot Spot Hot?

- There are beautiful landscapes in every direction.
- The relatively motorboat-free waters are ideal for canoeing and kayaking.
- During an evening paddle, enjoy an intimate opportunity to observe a loon.

**Address:** 960 Hwy 637, Killarney, ON
**GPS:** 46.01304; −81.40174
**Tel.:** (705) 287-2900
**Website:** www.ontarioparks .com/park/killarney

**Open year-round**

&#9855; (Check ahead)

Ontario is a wonderful place to explore natural areas, whether by hiking rugged trails, snow-shoeing frozen wetlands, driving country roads or just sitting in a quiet forest and letting nature come to you. But exploring by canoe or kayak presents another amazing perspective for the naturalist, and Killarney Provincial Park is the place to do it.

Killarney is primarily a wilderness park on the north shore of Georgian Bay, and its almost 50,000 hectares offer a picturesque view no matter where you turn. On the Georgian Bay edge, you can explore the smooth pink granite shoreline. In the interior, you can marvel at the rounded white hills of the La Cloche Mountains, dotted with mixed forests and cliff edges. And everywhere, there is clear, cobalt-blue water that makes you feel as though your boat is hovering rather than floating over the surface.

Canoeing or kayaking here affords an excellent chance to really observe Ontario's

official bird, the common loon. If you approach slowly and quietly, it's often possible to come close enough to hear the loon's quiet contact hoot or watch as it preens its dappled plumage. When the loon dives, you may briefly see it swim under water before it disappears into the lake's depths. Don't, however, approach a loon swimming with young or one that is clearly agitated, which is a good indication that you may be close to its shoreline nest. Stressing these birds causes them to lose valuable energy that they need to raise their families.

On land, take advantage of Killarney's many kilometres of trails for hiking and snowshoeing. The park is home to moose, deer, black bears, wolves and martens, as well as more than 100 species of breeding or nesting birds. As you wander the beautiful landscape, you'll have no trouble understanding why the Group of Seven artists were committed to convincing the Ontario government to make this a park in the first place.

←↑ **Come and float on the lakes in Killarney with the common loon, Ontario's provincial bird.**

# Lake Superior Provincial Park

by Tracy C. Read

***The shoreline of this wilderness park tells a haunting tale of human and geological history***

## What Makes This Hot Spot Hot?

- The Lake Superior shoreline in the park is a visual essay on the region's geological history.
- A short rugged path from Highway 17 takes you to one of the most visited pictograph sites in Canada, accessible on foot only when Superior is calm.
- The Trans-Canada Highway (Highway 17) bisects the park, which has 11 hiking trails and a wide selection of campsites.

**Address**: Lake Superior Provincial Park Visitor Centre, Hwy 17 N, Wawa, ON
**GPS**: 47.33588; –84.61598
**Tel.**: (705) 856-2284 (year-round); (705) 882-2026 (May to mid-October)
**Website**: www.ontarioparks.com/park/lakesuperior

**Open May to mid-October**

↗ **A sandy beach along the shoreline of the greatest of the Great Lakes.**

Over a billion years ago, tectonic plates shifted and fractured the continent's bedrock spine, producing a massive rift valley through the region that now includes Lake Superior. In time, volcanic and glacial activity filled the rift with a sequence of rocks until, after the last ice age, meltwaters created the greatest of the Great Lakes. Visitors to the shoreline in Lake Superior Provincial Park, which sprawls 1,550 square kilometres along the northeastern coast of Superior, will find vivid evidence of the lake's tumultuous origin.

At Agawa Bay, roam one of the longest beaches on Superior's north shore, built with sand and cobble swept here by the Agawa River from inland beach terraces over thousands of years. Note the water-scoured bedrock at the southern end of the beach, forged from basalt, granite and gneiss. Across the headland's outcrops run ancient fractures filled with minerals: A dark basaltic stripe is sandwiched between pink granite and grey gneiss; nearby, a stripe of white granite boldly snakes through a bed of gneiss. On a sun-soaked summer day,

it's a peaceful scene that belies a raucous history of ruptured landscapes and erupting molten rock.

There's a story of human history here as well. A short drive north of Agawa Bay on the Trans-Canada is the turnoff to the Agawa Rock pictographs. A trail descends through rock chasms and massive broken boulders to the lake, where a rock ledge runs along the base of a 30-metre-high vertical

↑ On a calm day, paddlers are able to access the Agawa Rock pictographs.

→ A centuries-old Ojibwe pictograph on the cliff face at Agawa Rock.

cliff. Here, roughly 400 years ago, Ojibwe recorded their daily lives, dreams and visions on the sheer face of this white crystalline granite using a mix of red ochre and clay. After centuries of sun, wind, waves and winter storms, these sacred paintings endure.

OUIMET CANYON PROVINCIAL PARK

# Ouimet Canyon

by Tracy C. Read

*Often called "Canada's Grand Canyon," Ouimet Canyon is a rare opportunity to experience a wall of rock with a sheer drop of 100 metres*

## What Makes This Hot Spot Hot?

- It's a rare opportunity to witness a sheer drop of 100 metres.
- The canyon features a massive rock column known as the Indian Head.
- Nearby privately owned Eagle Canyon Adventures boasts Canada's longest zip line and longest suspension footbridge.

**Address**: Greenwich Lake Rd, Pass Lake, ON
**GPS**: 48.78922; −88.67192
**Tel.**: (807) 977-2526
**Website**: www.ontarioparks .com/park/ouimetcanyon

**Open May to October**

 (Check ahead)

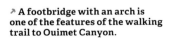
↗ **A footbridge with an arch is one of the features of the walking trail to Ouimet Canyon.**

There's no shortage of spectacular views for people travelling along the northern shoreline of Lake Superior, but there's unanimous agreement that a short detour leading to Ouimet Canyon is well worth taking. Less than an hour's drive northeast of Thunder Bay and about 15 kilometres off the Trans-Canada Highway (Highway 17), the 2-kilometre-long protected canyon, part of Ouimet Canyon Provincial Park, offers a rare glimpse into the region's geological past.

Ouimet Canyon was formed when the weight of glaciers and their meltwater split open the volcanic rock that characterizes Lake Superior's northern shore. The eroding effect of wind and rain over time has continued that work, as evidenced by the field of fallen rocks at the base of the canyon.

After a modest entrance fee and an easy hike in from the parking lot, visitors can take the measure of the 100-metre-deep, 150-metre-wide gorge from two viewing platforms

↑ **The sheer cliffs of Ouimet Canyon rise up from the rocky canyon floor.**

that are linked by a trail and boardwalk. The view across the canyon is of a vast rock cliff face shaped by the distinctive vertical joints of volcanic rock. To the north, the canyon winds its way into the hills that envelop the area. To the south, the canyon settles into a valley and a stunning wide-angle glimpse of Lake Superior. On an overcast day, the vista can take on an almost eerie, otherworldly atmosphere.

The virtually sunless, wind-free zone that exists at the canyon's ground floor offers up yet another intriguing feature. Here, as in the garden of Oscar Wilde's *Selfish Giant*, ice and snow persist most of the year, promoting the growth of vegetation that would otherwise grow only in Arctic and subarctic zones to the north. To preserve and protect this fragile plant ecosystem, visitors are not allowed to travel to the bottom of the canyon.

# Kakabeka Falls Provincial Park

by Tracy C. Read

*This picturesque 40-metre-high falls is truly the Niagara of the north*

## What Makes This Hot Spot Hot?

- Far from wax museums and food vendors, this wilderness waterfall has impressive offerings four seasons of the year.
- The park runs summertime programs through which visitors can learn about the area's geology and native wildlife and flora.
- The trails and viewing platforms are easily accessed and offer a variety of views.

**Address:** 4853 Trans-Canada Hwy (Hwy 17), Kakabeka Falls, ON
**GPS:** 48.40371; −89.62466
**Tel.:** (807) 473-9231
**Website:** www.ontarioparks .com/park/kakabekafalls

**Open year-round for day use; camping from May long weekend through Thanksgiving**

🔭 🚶 ⛺ 🚴 🏊 🚣 🏃

♿ (Check ahead)

↗ **A bald eagle cruises above the gorge, in search of spawning salmon.**

Just west of Thunder Bay, this 5-square-kilometre park embraces the thunderous waterfall named for the Ojibwe word *gakaabikaa*, which means "waterfall over a cliff." And fall Kakabeka does, as the iron-stained Kaministiquia River plunges 40 metres into a massive gorge carved from the underlying Precambrian Shield. Below the waterfall, the river flows through an expansive flood plain created after the last ice age.

While Kakabeka Falls is just off the Trans-Canada, it has none of the commercial trappings attached to its larger, citified southern cousin, Niagara. Apart from a visitor centre, boardwalk and viewing platforms, the park maintains an exhilarating wilderness setting. That makes it easy to imagine the wonder these powerful, churning waters must have inspired in the region's Indigenous population and the voyageurs who travelled these waterways much later.

Visitors are welcome to follow the boardwalk and pedestrian bridge that wrap around the top of the falls. From here, there's a magnificent view of the river, the waterfall and the unstable shale escarpments that line the gorge below. Access to the gorge itself is prohibited because of the rock's fragility, but encased within the eroding rock are 1.6-million-year-old fossils. In the autumn, bald eagles can be seen gliding along the gorge in search of salmon swimming upriver to spawn.

There are six park trails, one of which is a 1.25-kilometre scenic loop through woods that is part of a historic portage. Another features a steep hike down into the river

valley and offers a look at nearby picturesque Little Falls. The 4-kilometre Poplar Point Trail loop provides opportunities for wildlife spotting and birdwatching, and in fall, the golden colours of the aspen forest are striking. In winter, the trail is groomed for cross-country skiing.

A true northern Ontario wonder, Kakabeka Falls won't be anybody's second greatest disappointment.

↑ **The explosive Kakabeka Falls plunges 40 metres.**

← **A park boardwalk passes through a corridor of conifers.**

# Parc national du Mont-Orford

by Debbie Olsen

**The most southerly provincial park in Quebec is a year-round destination for nature lovers**

## What Makes This Hot Spot Hot?

- Forests, valleys, mountains and waterways provide habitat for a wide array of species and opportunities for a variety of outdoor pursuits.
- The park is home to several independently operated facilities, including a ski resort, a golf course, the Orford Music Academy and an adventure resort called Jouvence.
- The sugar maple forest puts on a blazing show of autumn colours.

**Address:** 200 ch. du Camping, Orford, QC
**GPS:** 45.32931; −72.19549
**Tel.:** (819) 843-9855
**Website:** www.sepaq.com /pq/mor

**Open year-round**

♿ **(Limited, check ahead)**

More than three-quarters of this provincial park, located 80 minutes southeast of Montreal, is covered in maple forest, a sight that is particularly beautiful in autumn. Birch, balsam, fir, red spruce and oak trees can also be found in Parc national de Mont-Orford, which is very diverse in both flora and fauna. A variety of landscapes and ecosystems lie within its 59.5 square kilometres, including the 853-metre-high Mount Orford Massif, for which the park is named.

Visitors can hike to the top of Mount Orford or take the gondola up and enjoy five lookout points at 850 metres. From the Memphrémagog Lookout, you can see beautiful Lake Memphrémagog in the distance. The lake has a surface area of more than 110 square kilometres and spans the U.S./Canada border.

Mount Orford is the park's highest peak. De l'Ours Peak (*pic de l'Ours* in French, which stands 740 metres high) and Mount Chauve (600 metres high) are the second- and third-tallest mountains in the park. They are all part of the Appalachian Mountains, which run from the southern United States all the way to Newfoundland.

Lake Fraser and Lake Stukely are two prime recreational spots in the park. Both lakes have lovely supervised beaches with playground facilities, picnic tables, convenience stores, boat rentals, toilets and campgrounds. At just over 4-square-kilometres, Stukely is the largest of the two lakes. It is also home to Jouvence (www.jouvence.com), an all-inclusive adventure resort that includes meals, accommodations and outdoor activities for its guests.

The wide variety of habitats in the park allows for a diversity of wildlife. Keep an eye out for white-tailed deer, moose, beavers, coyotes and river otters as you hike or cycle through the park. There are more than 80 kilometres of hiking trails, and in late September and early October, it's common to see newly hatched baby snapping turtles along park pathways. More

than 210 bird species have been identified in the park. Barred owls can be found in the park year-round and are its emblematic animal.

Parc national du Mont-Orford is a nature highlight of the Eastern Townships region of Quebec.

## Music in the Park

Orford Music Academy was founded in 1951 by Gilles Lefebvre with the support of Youth and Music Canada. It has since become one of the top summer music academies in North America. Every summer, the academy hosts the Orford Music Festival, a world-class event that attracts nearly 25,000 festival-goers. The festival features professional concerts, family-friendly activities, a visual art exhibition and a music competition.

↑ Hiking is at its best in the fall, when the forests are aflame with hues of yellow, orange and red.

↖ Mount Orford and Lake Stukely can be seen from the summit of Mount Chauve.

# Parc national de la Jacques-Cartier

by Debbie Olsen

**This beautiful 670-square-kilometre park is less than 30 minutes outside Quebec City**

## What Makes This Hot Spot Hot?

- At 550 metres deep, the Jacques-Cartier Valley is one of the most beautiful glacial valleys in Quebec.
- More than 100 kilometres of hiking trails and 30 kilometres of mountain biking trails showcase the park's scenic beauty.
- The Jacques-Cartier River allows canoeists and kayakers to explore the park as the first explorers did.

**Address**: 103 ch. du Parc-National, Stoneham-et-Tewkesbury, QC
**GPS**: 47.17443; −71.36989
**Tel.**: (418) 848-3169
**Website**: www.sepaq.com/pq/jac

**Open year-round**

⚕ (Check ahead)

The words "accessible" and "wilderness" don't often go together, but they do when you're talking about Parc national de la Jacques-Cartier. Less than a 30-minute drive from one of Canada's most beautiful and historic cities, this provincial park protects a region of the Laurentian Mountains that includes a vast plateau, deep valleys, stunning gorges and flowing rivers. It's a year-round outdoor paradise that is readily accessible from Quebec City, the provincial capital.

More than 200 lakes and several rivers run through the 670 square kilometres of this park. The Jacques-Cartier River and Valley are scenic highlights for which the park is named. Over many centuries, the river has cut a deep channel into the plateau, creating impressive tree-covered slopes.

The park has an excellent equipment rental program. During the summer and fall, visitors can rent canoes, kayaks, rafts, inner tubes, stand-up paddleboards and other equipment to explore the Jacques-Cartier River. First-timers can book a guided experience to learn how to read river rapids and manoeuvre a boat. Winter visitors can rent backcountry skis, "Hok" skis, snowshoes, fat bikes, electric fat bikes and kicksleds. There are no skate rentals, but the park has a 350-metre ice pathway that is illuminated in sections, so it can be used both in daylight hours and after dark. There's also a heated hut at Pôle Belleau (at kilometre 10).

A variety of campsites and comfort camping facilities are available. Ready-to-camp tents, yurts and cabins can be reserved for overnight stays, and there are packages that include accommodations and equipment rentals. First-time anglers can try their hand at catching speckled trout by booking a Ready-to-Fish

package that includes over-night cabin accommodations, a boat rental, fishing gear and a fishing access licence.

Hiking the trails is one of the best ways to explore Jacques-Cartier. There are more than 100 kilometres of hiking trails, including many with minimal elevation gain that are ideal for families. Les Loups Trail is one of the steeper uphill trails that is a must-do, especially in fall. Stunning views of yellow birch and sugar maple trees in the Jacques-Cartier and Sautauriski Valleys make the 4-hour return hike worth the effort. Le Scotora Trail is another great autumn hike that leads to a spectacular viewpoint at the summit of Andante Mountain (known as *mont Andante* in French).

While you explore, keep an eye out for moose; they are commonly seen in this park. White-tailed deer, grey wolves, red foxes, lynx, black bears, river otters, porcupines and beavers also live in the park. More than 169 bird species have been identified, including barred owls, bald eagles and ospreys.

Parc national de la Jacques-Cartier is a wilderness paradise that is beloved by Quebec's residents and visitors alike.

↑ **Red foxes are found in every province and territory in Canada.**

↖ **The tree-covered Jacques-Cartier Valley is particularly stunning in the fall.**

# Charlevoix Biosphere Reserve

by Debbie Olsen

**This UNESCO-recognized biosphere reserve covers 457,000 hectares bordering the north side of the St. Lawrence River and includes two provincial parks**

## What Makes This Hot Spot Hot?

- Parc national des Grands-Jardins and Parc national des Hautes-Gorges-de-la-Rivière-Malbaie are at the core of this biosphere reserve.
- The biosphere reserve contains many different ecosystems and diverse flora and fauna.
- The ecological centre of Port-au-Saumon offers natural science summer camps and educational interpretive programs.

**Address:** 63 rue Ambroise-Fafard, Baie-Saint-Paul, QC
**GPS:** 47.43845; –70.50614
**Tel.:** (418) 617-1979
**Website:** www.biospherecharlevoix.org

**Open year-round**

&#9855; (Check ahead)

Charlevoix is a beautiful region of Quebec, and this UNESCO-recognized biosphere covers a huge area that includes farmland, rivers, marine areas, tidal marshes, forests, stunted vegetation and mountains. At its heart are two provincial parks — Parc national des Grands-Jardins and Parc national des Hautes-Gorges-de-la-Rivière-Malbaie. Other outstanding facilities include the ecological centre of Port-au-Saumon and Palissades de Charlevoix. There are two ski resorts inside the biosphere and many other recreational facilities that support outdoor pursuits.

## Parc national des Grands-Jardins

Early 20th-century visitors to the area that is now Parc national des Grands-Jardins were so impressed by the exceptional vegetation that they named it *Grands Jardins*, which means "Great Gardens." Inside its 319 square kilometres are mountains, rivers, lakes and plateaus that were shaped by a meteorite impact some 400 million years ago and then reshaped by glaciers and time. The bodies of water in this park are renowned for speckled trout fishing, and anglers can fish in 60 different lakes and several rivers. The park offers boat rentals and free fishing equipment loans, so it's easy for novices and families to go fishing.

More than 30 kilometres of hiking trails traverse many different landscapes, from tundra to forest to mountains. As you hike through the park, keep an eye out for black bears, moose, woodland caribou, grey wolves, red foxes, porcupines, lynx and spruce grouse. The spruce grouse is the park's emblematic animal.

## Parc national des Hautes-Gorges-de-la-Rivière-Malbaie

One of the best ways to see the dramatic landscapes in this 224.7-square-kilometre park is on a 90-minute riverboat cruise of the Malbaie

→ **The Malbaie River cuts through verdant mountain scenery in Parc national des Hautes-Gorges-de-la-Rivière-Malbaie.**

River Valley. Parc national des Hautes-Gorges-de-la-Rivière-Malbaie has some of the highest rock walls east of the Rockies. It's a place where deep valleys are cut into steep mountains. More than 40 kilometres of trails lead to lookouts and nature sites.

It's common to see ospreys and great blue herons near the Malbaie River. Black bears, red foxes, beavers, muskrats, grey wolves, porcupines, river otters, martens and raccoons are among the many mammals that live in this park. Equipment rentals, interpretive programs, facilities and services, like a snow shuttle, make exploring this park enjoyable in every season.

## Ecological Centre of Port-au-Saumon

For more than 50 years, the ecological centre of Port-au-Saumon has been educating students and visitors about the region's fascinating forest and marine ecosystems. The centre offers educational programs and natural science summer camps. There are five different interpretive trails that can be accessed on scheduled guided hikes.

## Palissades de Charlevoix

A wide range of activities can be enjoyed at Palissades de Charlevoix. There are two *via ferrata* (protected climbing route) courses, a swinging bridge, climbing and rappelling facilities, and a double zip line. There are also 20 kilometres of marked hiking trails and several types of accommodations.

→ **Get your adrenaline pumping while conquering a *via ferrata* course at Palissades de Charlevoix.**

# Parc national de Miguasha

by Debbie Olsen

*This small park on the southern coast of the Gaspé Peninsula is a UNESCO World Heritage Site that contains the world's most outstanding collection of fossils from the Devonian period*

## What Makes This Hot Spot Hot?

- This site contains five of the six fossil fish groups associated with the Devonian period as well as the most and best-preserved fossils of lobe-finned fish on the planet.
- There are excellent interpretive programs and educational fossil displays.
- Visitors have the opportunity to take guided tours of an active fossil excavation site.

**Address**: 231 rte Miguasha Ouest, Nouvelle, QC
**GPS**: 48.10426; –66.34819
**Tel.**: (418) 794-2475
**Website**: www.sepaq.com /pq/mig/

**Open May through October**

& (Check ahead)

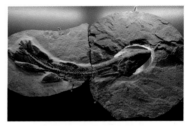

A 380-million-year-old fossil-rich cliff known as the Escuminac Formation is the focal point of Parc national de Miguasha, located at the western end of Chaleur Bay (*baie des Chaleurs* in French) on the Gaspé Peninsula. This site has been recognized by UNESCO as the world's most outstanding illustration of the Devonian period.

In the on-site natural history museum, you'll find magnificent permanent fossil displays. The most significant museum exhibit, *Origins of a Quest*, contains the only fully intact specimen of *Elpistostege watsoni* ever found in the world. Preliminary research on this fish fossil suggests it could be the closest relative to tetrapods — vertebrates with legs. Nicknamed "Elpi," this fossil is a key piece of the evolutionary biology puzzle.

More than 14,000 specimens of fish, plants and invertebrates have been extracted from the Escuminac Formation. If you happen to visit on Quebec National Parks Day,

you can take a tour of the research centre, the only facility of its kind in the Quebec parks network. In the labs, scientists prepare, catalogue and study fossil specimens from the cliff. On-site collection rooms allow scientists to store and protect the fossils.

↗ **The specimens in the on-site museum paint a vivid picture of life during the Upper Devonian period.**

There are hands-on displays, including an outdoor fossil sandbox where children can pretend to be paleontologists extracting Miguasha fish fossils. In July and August there is a puppet show designed for younger guests, but it is only available in French. Interpretive programming has been adapted for visitors of all ages, and most programs are offered in both French and English.

The highlight of this park is the chance to visit the fossil cliff, an active excavation site. You can visit the cliff on your own, but a guided tour with a park interpreter will provide more information on the geology of the area and how fossils are extracted from the site. You may see fossils among the stones on the beach, but you cannot remove them as the law forbids the collection of rock samples within the park.

After visiting the fossil cliff, wander along the 3.5-kilometre Evolution of Life interpretive trail loop, which runs through a treed area along the top of the cliff. Interpretive panels provide information about the evolution of life on Earth, and the trail offers nice views of the Restigouche River Estuary.

With a total area of just 0.8 square kilometres, this park is the smallest in Quebec's parks system, but it packs a big punch.

# Parc national de l'Île-Bonaventure-et-du-Rocher-Percé

by Debbie Olsen

**This unique park at the tip of the Gaspé Peninsula is a bird-lovers paradise that is home to one of Quebec's iconic natural symbols**

## What Makes This Hot Spot Hot?

- Legendary Percé Rock is one of the world's largest water-based natural arches and an icon of Quebec.
- This park is home to the largest migratory bird refuge in North America.
- Bonaventure Island's colony of 110,000 northern gannets is the most accessible in the world.

**Address:** 4 rue du Quai, Percé, QC
**GPS:** 48.52192; −64.21311
**Tel.:** (418) 782-2240
**Websites:** www.sepaq.com /pq/bon

**Open mid-May to mid-October**

♿ (Limited, check ahead)

Rising out of the water like a massive ship under sail, Percé Rock (known as *Rocher Percé* in French) has become an iconic symbol of Quebec's Gaspésie region. In French, the name means "pierced rock." It refers to the 15-metre-high and 30-metre-wide arch on the seaward end of this massive monolith. Once connected to the mainland, Percé Rock stands alone at 433 metres long, 90 metres wide and 88 metres high. It's only connection to the Gaspésie coast is a sandbar visible at low tide. The limestone rock provides a home to many species of birds and is a breeding site for cormorants and black-legged kittiwakes.

Forces of erosion have greatly changed Percé Rock over time. When French explorer Jacques Cartier arrived at Gaspé Bay on July 24, 1534, the rock had three arches. It's unknown when the third arch disappeared, but the second one collapsed on June 17, 1845. Ice protects the rock from the wind and waves of winter storms, but the warming climate has decreased the density and duration of the ice. Some experts believe the

remaining arch will disappear in about 400 years.

A boat tour is the best way to get a close look at Percé Rock and to visit nearby Bonaventure Island. The tours run several times daily, weather permitting. Many different bird species and a variety of marine life can be viewed from the boat. At Bonaventure Island, you can get off and hike the trails, explore historical buildings and see wildlife.

Bonaventure Island is a birding paradise. More than 200,000 birds nest on the 4.16-square-kilometre island, including 110,000 northern gannets. Visitors can get very close to the gannet colony, which is by far the world's most accessible colony and the real highlight of the park. Four hiking trails lead visitors through fields, meadows and forests to the gannet colony. Park wardens at the colony are also naturalists and can answer questions about the birds and other wildlife.

Park wardens lead a variety of interpretive activities on Bonaventure Island as well as Discovery Evenings at La Saline Performance Hall in the small city of Percé. History lovers will enjoy exploring Le Boutillier House on Bonaventure Island and Le Chafaud Discovery Centre in Percé. You'll learn about the park's history, fauna, flora and geology as well as the history of the fishing industry in the Gaspésie region.

If you aren't a bird lover before visiting this unique park, you will be when you leave. Observing northern gannets, the park's emblematic animal, is a fascinating and educational experience.

↑ Birders can get up close and personal with Bonaventure Island's gannet colony.

← The distinct profile of Percé Rock is hard to miss.

↓ Northern gannets return to Bonaventure Island every summer to breed, and each pair raises one chick per summer.

# Forillon National Park

by Debbie Olsen

**The first federal national park in Quebec protects the flora and fauna of the cliffs, forests, coast, salt marshes, sand dunes and mountains as well as significant historical sites**

## What Makes This Hot Spot Hot?

- The park's jaw-dropping scenery can be enjoyed from unique viewpoints like Land's End.
- Minke whales, humpback whales, fin whales and blue whales frequent the waters surrounding the park.
- Cliffs provide habitat for tens of thousands of seabirds, including the largest black-legged kittiwake colony in eastern Canada.

**Address:** 1238 boul. de Forillon, Gaspé, QC
**GPS:** 48.85603; −64.41248
**Tel.:** (418) 368-5505
**Website:** www.pc.gc.ca/en /pn-np/qc/forillon/index

Open year-round; park entrances open late-May to mid-October, and visitor centres open mid-June to mid-October

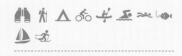

&#9855; (Check ahead)

The Mi'kmaq called the farthest point of land on the peninsula that juts into the Gulf of St. Lawrence *Gespeg*, which means "where the land ends." Today, Land's End is one of the most stunningly beautiful spots in Forillon National Park — a place where ocean views literally take your breath away. The French names *Gaspé* and *Gaspésie*, which are used for the peninsula and the region, respectively, are also likely derived from the same Mi'kmaq word.

Forillon's sheer cliffs offer breathtaking viewpoints, but they also provide important habitat for tens of thousands of seabirds, including the largest black-legged kittiwake colony in eastern Canada. Many other seabirds — like razorbills, common murres, double-crested cormorants, black guillemots, great black-backed gulls and herring gulls — make the cliffs their home. There's also an abundance of terrestrial birds. Some 246 species, including 125 nesting varieties, have been spotted in the

→ The Cape Gaspé Lighthouse stands at the tip of the Forillon Peninsula and overlooks Gaspé Bay.

⦓ Forillon National Park is bursting with breathtaking panoramas of forests, cliffs and ocean.

⦔ Forillon National Park is home to a large population of porcupines.

park. Among these are many raptor species, such as ospreys, northern harriers, kestrels and rough-legged hawks.

Located at the extreme northeast end of Quebec's Gaspé Peninsula, the 244-square-kilometre park preserves a wide range of habitats. The waters surrounding the peninsula teem with life, and the park includes a narrow strip of marine area that runs along the coast. It's common to see seals, dolphins and whales, including endangered species like the harbour porpoise, the fin whale and the blue whale, on a boat tour.

Forty-three species of mammals are found in the park. Moose, black bears, coyotes, lynx, porcupines, beavers, red foxes, snowshoe hares and red squirrels are just a few animals that visitors might see while hiking the trails.

You can also explore five fascinating heritage sites in Forillon. A visit to Dolbel-Roberts House, Blanchette House, Hyman & Sons General Store or the Cape Gaspé Lighthouse lets you step back in time

to the days when commercial cod fishing was the main industry in the region. At Fort Peninsula's underground fortifications, you can tour a fully preserved World War II coastal battery and learn about the role the Gaspé naval base played in the Battle of St. Lawrence.

There's lots to love about Forillon National Park. Be sure to take in the view from Cap Bon-Ami, preferably at sunrise. It's something that will stay with you long after you leave.

# Mingan Archipelago National Park Reserve

by Debbie Olsen

**The 20 main islands and nearly 1,000 smaller islands and islets of this archipelago tell a fascinating geological story**

## What Makes This Hot Spot Hot?

- The park is home to the largest concentration of erosion monoliths in Canada.
- A wide array of seabirds, including puffins, razorbills, guillemots, eiders, terns and kittiwakes, nest on the islands.
- The park's sedimentary rock formations date back more than 450 million years.

**Address:** 1010 Prom. des Anciens, Havre-Saint-Pierre, QC
**GPS:** 50.23683; –63.60632
**Tel.:** (418) 538-3285 (Havre-Saint-Pierre Reception and Interpretation Centre)
**Websites:** www.pc.gc.ca/en/pn-np/qc/mingan/index

**Open early June to late September; opening times for reception and interpretation centres and reception kiosks vary**

&#9855; (Check ahead)

If you get the feeling there's something primeval about the sculpted limestone monoliths that stretch as far as the eye can see in this federal national park, you're right. The park's dramatic sedimentary rock formations date back more than 450 million years, to a time when an ancient sea covered the St. Lawrence Lowlands. Over millions of years, continental shift and the incredible power of natural erosion have shaped the striking landscape you see today.

Each island in the 110 square kilometres of Mingan Archipelago National Park Reserve is unique, and you should plan to do some island hopping. Local boat and ferry operators offer a variety of cruises and stopover services, which will help you see the main sites.

The islands that make up this unique national park contain a great diversity of habitats, plants and animal species. Peat bogs, salt marshes, boreal forests, barrens and many kilometres of shoreline make up this park reserve, and visitors can discover more than 450 species of vascular plants, almost 190 species of lichen and more than 300 species of moss within its boundaries. The park contains many rare plants and even some species that are listed as both rare and endangered, such as the Mingan thistle. Hikers should stay on marked trails or accessible natural beaches to avoid harming delicate plants.

Approximately 35,000 nesting pairs of seabirds from 12 different species occupy the islands during breeding season. Of these, the Atlantic puffin is the most sought-after sighting for most visitors. These colourful birds are sometimes called "sea parrots" (*perroquets de mer* in French), because of their brightly coloured beaks, and in French they're also often called *calculots*, meaning "counters," because of the way they nod

repeatedly, like a person counting. You can find puffins on these three Mingan islands from mid-April to early September: Île de la Maison, Île à Calculot des Betchouanes and Île aux Perroquets. Despite the name, the smallest population of puffins is found on Île aux Perroquets.

There's also an abundance of marine life in the Mingan Archipelago. On the beaches and in the waters near the islands you can see grey seals, harbour seals and harp seals. Minke whales and common porpoises frequent the waters near the islands, and blue whales, humpback whales and fin whales can be found in deeper waters, farther from land.

Birds are the definite wildlife highlight of these islands, but you may also see land mammals such as beavers, river otters, muskrats, snowshoe hares and red and silver foxes. Black bears and moose have occasionally been seen on islands closer to the coast.

Mingan Archipelago National Park Reserve is remote, but it's worth the effort to get there. It's a place unlike anywhere else on the planet.

↑ An Atlantic puffin carries sandeels in its beak. Sandeels are a staple food for feeding puffin chicks.

↖ These massive limestone outcroppings are distinctive features of Mingan Archipelago National Park Reserve.

Labrador City

Happy Valley-Goose Bay

**12**

Labrador

Quebec

St. Lawrence River

Quebec

Gulf of St. Lawrence

Corner Brook

**10**

Newfou

New Brunswick

Prince Edward Island

**7**

**4**

Summerside

**8** **9**

Charlottetown

Moncton

Sydney

105

Fredericton

USA

Saint John

**2** **3**

Truro

**6**

**1**

Nova Scotia

**5**

Halifax

102

104

104

104

105

N

W    E

S

Atl

Labrador
Sea

# Atlantic Canada

## New Brunswick

## Nova Scotia

## Prince Edward Island

## Newfoundland and Labrador

Grand
Falls

•Gander

•St. John's

# Grand Manan Archipelago

By Debbie Olsen

**The islands of this archipelago are a spectacular birding destination that is also filled with uncrowded beaches, quaint fishing villages and wonderful hiking trails**

## What Makes This Hot Spot Hot?

- The Grand Manan Archipelago is an important bird area that is renowned for birdwatching.
- Close to 100 kilometres of hiking trails provide opportunities for viewing seabirds, coastline and lighthouses.
- These isolated islands have interesting flora and fauna and do not contain any predatory land animals.

**Address:** 130 Rte 776, Grand Manan, NB
**GPS:** 44.76554; −66.75883
**Tel.:** (888) 525-1655
**Website:** www.grandmanannb.com

**Open year-round; no ferry service on Christmas Day**

♿ (Check ahead)

The Grand Manan Archipelago has been renowned as a bird-watching destination since John James Audubon visited in 1831. There are 20 islands in the archipelago, but at just over 655 square kilometres, Grand Manan Island is the largest. Deer Island, the Wolves Archipelago, Campobello Island, White Head Island and Machias Seal Island are some of the other main islands in the group, which together comprise the most southerly region of New Brunswick. In fact, Machias Seal Island and North Rock are so close to the U.S. border that there have been disputes over which country they belong to. Canada has maintained a staffed lighthouse at Machias Seal since 1832, supporting its claim to the island.

Situated on the western side of the mouth of the Bay of Fundy, the islands are subject to the forces of the world's highest tides. They also lie along a major eastern flyway, which accounts for the incredible number of bird species that can be seen. Together the islands have an incredible diversity of habitats that support a vast number of birds, a wide array of marine mammals and some land animals. Since Grand Manan is a 90-minute ferry ride from the mainland, only species capable of swimming or flying across 32 kilometres of ocean live here, and there are no predatory land mammals.

Birding can be enjoyed year-round on these islands, and thousands of razorbills, common murres, kittiwakes and dovekies can be seen in the winter months. The peak seasons for most birders, however, are the spring migration, summer nesting period and fall migration. More than 360 bird species have been identified, with some 131 known to nest in the archipelago. Boat tours can be arranged to visit the nesting seabird colony on Machias Seal Island. A limited number of people can visit the island each day to get close-up views of nesting seabirds, such as Atlantic puffins, Arctic terns,

razorbills and common murres.

Finback, humpback, minke and endangered North Atlantic right whales can be seen in the waters surrounding the islands. Whale watching tours often develop into birdwatching tours as well. Thousands of pelagic birds feed in the waters just off the islands, including red-necked phalaropes and several species of storm-petrel.

On the islands, nearly 100 kilometres of trails lead to lighthouses, fishing villages, two migratory bird sanctuaries, three nature preserves, Anchorage Provincial Park and Castalia Marsh. Indoors, you can catch a glimpse of island life at the Grand Manan Museum and see over 300 taxidermy birds in the Allan Moses Gallery.

The Grand Manan Archipelago is a nature lover's dream destination. Make sure to give yourself plenty of time to explore this unique corner of Canada.

↑ Charming Atlantic Puffins can be spotted on Machias Seal Island.

↖ The cliffs along the Southwest Head of Grand Manan Island are made up of columnar basalt.

# Fundy National Park

by Debbie Olsen

***Created in 1948, New Brunswick's first national park offers many outdoor activities, wonderful hiking trails and stunning coastal views***

## What Makes This Hot Spot Hot?

- This park is at the heart of the UNESCO-designated Fundy Biosphere Reserve.
- More than 100 kilometres of hiking trails traverse a wide variety of terrain, from mountains to waterfalls to stunning coastline shaped by the world's highest tides.
- The park is home to some 815 species of vascular plants, including the rare birdeye primrose, which is found nowhere else in New Brunswick.

**Address**: 8642 Rte 114, Alma, NB
**GPS**: 45.59543; −64.95083
**Tel.**: (506) 887-6000
**Website**: www.pc.gc.ca/en /pn-np/nb/fundy/index

**Open year-round; visitor services available January to October**

&#9855; **(Check ahead)**

The 206 square kilometres of Fundy National Park are an outdoor adventure wonderland. You can experience the Bay of Fundy's incredible tides in a kayak, on an interpretive walk on the tidal flats or on the spectacular Fundy Coastal Drive, which runs through this national park. Or you might prefer to venture inland on a hiking trail and discover a vibrant green forest, lovely lakes, several rivers and numerous waterfalls.

The park is situated on the Atlantic bird migration route, and more than 260 bird species have been reliably identified inside its boundaries. Warblers, pileated woodpeckers, ruffed grouse, juncos, white-winged crossbills, great blue herons, cormorants and shorebirds are commonly seen.

Peregrine falcons might also be seen soaring along the Fundy coast. These birds are one of the park's success stories. Once plentiful, they had completely disappeared by the time the national park was established. The species was reintroduced in the 1980s and is now thriving in near record numbers.

The park is home to other rare species as well, such as the eastern waterfan

(*Peltigera hydrothyria*), a species of aquatic lichen that has been designated threatened under the Species at Risk Act (SARA). Fundy National Park actually has more than 50 per cent of the Canadian population of this rare lichen within its boundaries.

Among the 815 species of vascular plants is the rare birdeye primrose (*Primula laurentiana*), a flowering plant that is found nowhere else in New Brunswick. The plant established itself in the area after glaciers melted millions of years ago.

There are also two uncommon species of salamanders here: Fundy is the only Canadian national park known to have northern dusky salamanders and the only place in New Brunswick where you can find four-toed salamanders. Other animals commonly seen include moose, white-tailed deer, eastern coyotes, beavers, snowshoe hares, chipmunks and red squirrels.

In 2011 Fundy National Park was designated a Dark Sky Preserve by the Royal Astronomical Society of Canada. There is very little artificial light within the park, making it a great place for stargazing. It's also a haven for nocturnal species like mice, shrews, northern saw-whet owls and northern flying squirrels, which are almost as plentiful as red squirrels in the park.

Whether you are paddling on Bennett or Wolfe Lakes, walking on the tidal flats near Alma Beach at low tide or hiking to a stunning waterfall, you'll love exploring Fundy National Park, and you'll find warm hospitality in the communities that surround it.

↑ The trail to Laverty Falls takes hikers through a mixed forest of maple, birch and beech.

← The lookout from Dickson Falls offers a breathtaking view of the land and sea that makes up this unique national park.

↓ An inner Bay of Fundy Atlantic salmon swims in the Upper Salmon River. This species is endangered and the focus of a decades-long recovery project.

# Hopewell Rocks Provincial Park

by Debbie Olsen

**_Over thousands of years, powerful tides in the Bay of Fundy have carved a remarkable landscape that can be explored on foot at low tide_**

## What Makes This Hot Spot Hot?

- Visitors can walk on the ocean floor among giant rock formations at this unique park.
- The interpretive centre and its staff teach lessons on local geology, tides, wildlife and history.
- From mid-July to mid-August, hundreds of thousands of migrating shorebirds pass through the park.

**Address**: 131 Discovery Rd, Hopewell Cape, NB
**GPS**: 45.81815; −64.57816
**Tel.**: (506) 734-3429;
(877) 734-3429
**Website**:
www.thehopewellrocks.ca

**Open mid-May to mid-October**

&#9855; **(Check ahead)**

About 160 billion metric tons of water flows in and out of the Bay of Fundy twice each day, and it is the force of these incredible tides that has carved the famous flowerpot-shaped rock formations near Hopewell Cape. The tallest formations are 21 metres high. They were nicknamed the Flowerpots because of the way they look at low tide: The trees and shrubs that grow on top of the brown rock formations look much like plants growing in a clay pot. At low tide, it's possible to view the formations from the ground up by walking along 2 kilometres of beach and exploring the coves. At high tide, a guided sea kayak excursion provides an entirely different perspective.

There is something otherworldly about this landscape. The Mi'kmaq have many traditional stories about this part of Canada. One tells of Mi'kmaq people who were enslaved by great whales that once lived in the Bay of Fundy. When tides were low, the slaves saw a chance for escape, but they were not fast enough. The angry whales turned them all to stone, and their spirits were trapped in the rock pillars.

Even today, people see familiar shapes in the rock formations. Pareidolia is so accepted here that many of the rocks have nicknames inspired by their appearance: Lover's Arch, Dinosaur Rock, Mother-in-Law and ET are just a few of the names for specific formations.

Erosion is constantly shaping and changing this landscape. New pillars are formed as the cliffs along the shore erode, and older pillars eventually wash away. In 2016, Elephant Rock, one of the most photographed rock formations, sheared almost in half. Roughly 100 to 200 metric tons of rock fell to the ground, closing off a passageway along the beach and dramatically changing the appearance of the formation.

↑ **Peregrine falcons are known to nest in the area around Hopewell Rocks.**

↑ **Visitors will have vastly different experiences of Hopewell Rocks at low and high tide.**

Geology is the big attraction at this provincial park, but you might also see wildlife. White-tailed deer, moose, raccoons, porcupines, rabbits, red foxes, coyotes and black bears are common in the area. Nearby Grindstone Island has a large nesting population of great blue herons, and they are commonly seen along with peregrine falcons, bald eagles, merlins, ospreys, cormorants and eiders. From mid-July to mid-August, you can see hundreds of thousands of migrating shorebirds. There are 34 different species, but semipalmated sandpipers, least sandpipers, short-billed dowitchers, semipalmated plovers, black-bellied plovers, red knots, white-rumped sandpipers, sanderlings and dunlins are the most common.

Hopewell Rocks Provincial Park is one of New Brunswick's top tourist attractions — and for good reason. Its natural wonders are unique and stunningly beautiful.

# Kouchibouguac National Park

by Debbie Olsen

*Stretching along the scenic Acadian coast, this park protects sand dunes, salt marshes, sandy beaches, lagoons and forests*

## What Makes This Hot Spot Hot?

- This park showcases the region's long history with Mi'kmaq and Acadian Peoples.
- The area provides habitat for endangered piping plovers and contains the second-largest common tern colony in North America.
- Kouchibouguac is a dark sky preserve that offers wonderful night sky viewing.

**Address:** 186 Rte 117, Kouchibouguac, NB
**GPS:** 46.77258; −65.00548
**Tel.:** (506) 876-2443
**Website:** www.pc.gc.ca/en/pn -np/nb/kouchibouguac/index

**Open year-round; visitor centre open mid-May to late-October**

♿ (Check ahead)

↗ **Bald eagles, which are endangered in New Brunswick, are sacred animals in Mi'kmaq culture.**

This park bears the Mi'kmaq name originally given to the Kouchibouguac River. It means "river of the long tides" and is pronounced "koo-shee-boo-gwack." The lands inside the park lie within the traditional territory of the Mi'kmaq, and archeological evidence shows human activity dating back about 4,000 years. This heritage is celebrated in the park's interpretive programs and in an annual *mawiomi*, or "gathering." The event includes ceremonies, prayers, traditional music and dance, storytelling, art, food and games.

Acadians also have strong ties to this land. When the national park was founded in 1969, there were seven Acadian communities — totalling about 1,200 people — inside its 238 square kilometres. All of their properties were expropriated to create the park. You can learn about their lives and their ties to the land in fascinating displays inside the visitor information centre.

Kouchibouguac National Park is an excellent destination for birdwatching, as it

contains a diverse range of habitats, from salt marshes to boreal forests and bogs. The endangered piping plover nests inside the park, and North America's second-largest common tern colony nests on the Tern Islands, which are part of the park. Large numbers of migrating shorebirds can be seen in the salt marshes, including short-billed dowitchers, sandpipers, red knots and Hudsonian godwits. Nelson's sparrows nest in the marshes, and northern gannets fish offshore. In the forests and spruce bogs, you might see woodpeckers, warblers, chickadees, owls, hawks, bald eagles, Canada jays and other species.

This park is popular with families and has excellent facilities. Kellys Beach is one of Canada's warmest salt-water beaches. It's a great place to swim and relax on a sunny summer day, and the sunsets are incredible. A 1-kilometre interpretive boardwalk provides access to the supervised beach and protects barrier dunes and other sensitive habitats.

Paddling is how the Mi'kmaq explored the area for thousands of years, and it's still a great way to see the park. There are two backcountry campgrounds for canoe camping. Canoes, kayaks, pedal boats, paddleboards and bicycles can be rented at Ryans Equipment Rental, or you can sign up for a voyageur canoe experience at the visitor information centre.

The park also has an excellent trail system. There are 60 kilometres of cycling trails, a 6.3-kilometre mountain bike trail and a groomed trail for fat biking in winter. The park's 10 hiking trails are suitable for hikers of all levels. While you're exploring, keep an eye out for land mammals like moose, raccoons, bobcats, lynx, wolves, coyotes, black bears, martens, porcupines, muskrats, beavers, woodchucks and snowshoe hares.

Kouchibouguac National Park is a special place. As you explore, you'll realize why it means so much to the people who have called it home.

⬆ The interpretive signs along Kellys Beach Boardwalk will teach you about the evolution of the barrier island dunes and the delicate ecology of the area.

⬇ Stargazers observe the clear night skies atop the Bog Trail tower.

# Kejimkujik National Park and National Historic Site

by Debbie Olsen

**This site has abundant wildlife, historic petroglyphs that date back thousands of years and white sand beaches along the stretch of coastline at Kejimkujik Seaside.**

## What Makes This Hot Spot Hot?

- With 46 lakes and ponds and 30 streams and rivers, this park offers some of the best paddling in Atlantic Canada.
- More than 500 petroglyphs provide clues to the human history of this area.
- The park is designated a dark sky preserve and offers guided experiences in July and August and a special "dark sky weekend" each summer.

**Address**: 3005 Kejimkujik Main Pkwy, Maitland Bridge, NS
**GPS**: 44.43841; −65.20855
**Tel.**: (902) 682-2772
**Website**: www.pc.gc.ca/en /pn-np/ns/kejimkujik/index

**Inland park open year-round; camping and visitor facilities open mid-May to late October; Kejimkujik National Park Seaside open seasonally with limited services**

&#9855; (Check ahead)

There are two separate land areas in this unique park: a 404-square-kilometre forested inland area that includes the Kejimkujik National Historic Site, and a separate 22-square-kilometre area along the Atlantic coast called Kejimkujik National Park Seaside, which features beautiful white sand beaches, coastal bogs and lagoons.

## Kejimkujik National Park and National Historic Site

For thousands of years, the Mi'kmaq experienced the natural wonders of this special place, and today visitors can connect with their culture and history through unique interpretive programs and by visiting ancient petroglyphs (rock carvings). More than 500 petroglyphs can be found along the lakeshores of Kejimkujik. It is one of the largest collections of rock art in eastern North America, and it tells a fascinating story.

The park offers unique guided cultural programs to help visitors discover Mi'kmaq culture, traditions and language. You can take a guided tour of the petroglyphs, sign up for a birchbark canoe building workshop, visit a recreated Mi'kmaq encampment, enjoy an outdoor theatre production or join a Parks Canada cultural guide for an evening of stargazing and storytelling. Each experience provides insights into the culture and traditions of the first people who lived on this land.

This national park is named for Kejimkujik Lake. The name is derived from the Mi'kmaq word *kejimkuji'jk*, which means "little fairies." Historically, the lake was known as Fairy Lake, and to this day one of its bays is called Fairy Bay. The Mi'kmaq have traditional stories involving little gnome-like people, which some believe are represented in the

petroglyphs near the lake.

This part of the park offers some of the best paddling in Canada along waterways in the Mersey River Watershed that the Mi'kmaq have traversed for thousands of years. Kejimkujik's on-site outfitter, Whynot Adventure (located at Jake's Landing), offers rental equipment and a shuttle service. The park has several backcountry campsites for canoe camping.

## Kejimkujik National Park Seaside

The white sands of St. Catherines River Beach and the turquoise waters that surround it are the highlights of this region of the park. Two scenic trails lead to secluded

coves, delicate dunes and an isolated shoreline, including one of the last undisturbed nesting beaches of the endangered piping plover. Along the coast, watch for harbour and grey seals and seabirds like eiders and cormorants. As you hike the interpretive trail, look out for wild orchids.

⬆ **Kejimkujik National Park Seaside is a naturalist's oasis, with plenty of flora and fauna to spot on both land and sea.**

⬉ **A paddle down the Mersey River is especially inviting during the fall.**

# Burntcoat Head Park

by Debbie Olsen

*This spot in the Bay of Fundy's Minas Basin holds the official Guinness World Record for the highest tides*

## What Makes This Hot Spot Hot?

- An incredible landscape carved by the world's highest tides can be seen and explored here.
- Tidal pools and tidal flats teem with life.
- A replica lighthouse contains an interpretive centre with information about the tides, past lighthouses and the history of the Minas Basin area.

**Address:** 45 Faulkner Ln, Noel, NS
**GPS:** 45.3110348, −63.8082489
**Tel.:** (902) 369-2529
**Website:** www.burntcoatheadpark.ca

**Open mid-May to early October**

&#9855; **(Limited, check ahead)**

↗ **During low tide at Burntcoat Head Park, visitors can walk on the ocean floor and peer into tidal pools.**

→ **Naturalists young and old can explore the tidal pools at low tide and discover everything from molluscs like razor clams and slipper limpets, to crustaceans like hermit crabs and toad crabs.**

At one time, this small 1.2-hectare park had a tide gauge operated by the Canadian Hydrographic Service. It was this tide gauge that accurately recorded the highest tidal range in the world, which was recognized in the *Guinness Book of World Records* in 1975.

Tides at Burntcoat Head average 14.5 metres, with the highest on record at 16.3 meters, recorded in 1975. The high tides combined with storm surges during the 1869 Saxby Gale brought water levels to an estimated 21.6 metres. These tides are incredible when you consider that the tidal range in much of the world is only about 1 metre.

About 160 billion metric tons of water flows into the Bay of Fundy twice a day, every day. To put this into perspective, it would take one year and nine months of continuously flowing water at Niagara Falls to equal 160 billion tons. This tremendous amount of tidal flow shapes the landscape and creates fascinating geological formations.

Visitors to Burntcoat Head should try to see it at both high tide and low tide. There's about 6 hours between high and low tide, and tidal charts are available on the website. Between tides, you can explore attractions in the park and neighbouring communities like Maitland, which is home to the Fundy Tidal Interpretive Centre and the Lawrence House Museum.

The Flying Apron Inn & Cookery in nearby Summerville is a fantastic stop for lunch or dinner, but if you want a truly unique experience inside the park, book one of their "Dining on the Ocean Floor" dinners at Burntcoat Head Park. These multi-course meals are held at low tide on long tables and feature gourmet food with craft beer and wine pairings. The experience includes a private tour of the park.

Even though the park is small, there are quite a few resident birds, such as pileated woodpeckers, flickers, yellow-bellied sapsuckers, ring-necked pheasants, goldfinches, bald eagles and the occasional osprey. Many

migratory shorebirds can be seen at certain times of the year, including sandpipers, whimbrels, plovers, yellow-legs, willets and turnstones.

Be sure to explore the trails and gardens in the park, walk on the ocean floor at low tide and visit the replica light-house, which also serves as an interpretive centre and gift shop. You'll learn more about the tides, the original lighthouses and the history of the Minas Basin. There's a lot to like and to learn in this tiny Bay of Fundy park.

# Cape Breton Highlands National Park

by Debbie Olsen

*This park is home to some of the prettiest coastal views in Canada*

## What Makes This Hot Spot Hot?

- Saltwater and freshwater beaches are great for swimming, walking and enjoying the sunset.
- Numerous hiking trails, 26 in all, lead to breathtaking locations in this park.
- About one-third of the world-famous Cabot Trail winds through this national park.

**Address:** 16648 Cabot Trail, Chéticamp, NS
**GPS:** 46.6464; −60.95053
**Tel.:** (902) 224-2306
**Website:** www.pc.gc.ca/en /pn-np/ns/cbreton/index

**Open mid-May to late October**

♿ (Check ahead)

↗ **The Skyline Trail is a highlight of the park, and is especially picturesque at sunset.**

The word "breathtaking" has new meaning when you're standing on the Skyline Trail platform overlooking the rugged coast of Cape Breton Island. From this viewpoint, it's easy to see why they describe this national park as "where the mountains meet the sea." In the distance, you can see the legendary Cabot Trail winding its way along the cliffs. It's one of the most famous drives in Canada for good reason.

Cape Breton Highlands National Park is a place that is completely unique in Canada. The coast and the highlands are the scenic highlights of the park. In the highlands, you'll find steep cliffs, deep river canyons and old-growth forests. The cool maritime climate supports a special mix of northern and southern species — including a few dozen rare and threatened plants and animals.

At 950 square kilometres, Cape Breton Highlands National Park is one of the largest protected wilderness areas in Nova Scotia. Vegetation in the park can be divided into three distinct land regions: Acadian, boreal and taiga. Acadian refers to mixed-wood forests like sugar maple, yellow birch, American beech and Dutchman's beech. Boreal refers to northern softwoods like balsam fir, white birch and black spruce. Taiga is characterized by scrub forest, barrens and bogs. This unique range of habitats supports 78 rare vascular plants and 29 rare moss and liverwort species.

The park also teems with wildlife. Odds are good that you'll see moose, and coyotes, snowshoe hares, white-tailed deer, black bears and lynx also call the park home. You can find brook trout, speckled trout and Atlantic salmon in the park's lakes and streams. In the waters surrounding the park, you might see marine species like harbour seals as well as minke, humpback and pilot whales. Watch for seabirds along the coast,

such as gulls, cormorants and guillemots, and bald eagles and hawks. You can see songbirds, grouse, owls and more in the forested areas of the park and from the trails.

There are many scenic viewpoints along the Cabot Trail where you can pull your vehicle over and take in the view, but the best vistas can be enjoyed from the trails. There are 26 different trails that lead to beautiful locations, many with secluded picnic spots. You can join an interpretive guided hike or explore on your own. The park has developed award-winning interpretive programming that allows guests to immerse themselves in nature and discover Mi'kmaq, Acadian and Celtic cultures.

There's much to see and do in Cape Breton Highlands National Park, and you can't beat the friendly hospitality in this part of Nova Scotia. Whether you're cycling, paddling, hiking or driving, you'll love exploring this beautiful part of Canada.

↓ Despite being a boreal species, moose are found in all three land regions in Cape Breton Highlands National Park.

# Cabot Beach Provincial Park

by Debbie Olsen

*Red cliffs surround a lovely swimming beach with day-use facilities and a campground on the western side of the island*

## What Makes This Hot Spot Hot?

- This park has a supervised swimming beach with excellent facilities, including a beach mat and a floating chair for guests with accessibility needs.
- There is a historic lighthouse as well as the historic Fanning School.
- Interpretive programming both entertains and educates visitors.

**Address:** 449 King St, Rte 20, Malpeque, PE
**GPS:** 46.5582; −63.70633
**Tel.:** (902) 836-8945
**Website:** www.tourismpei .com/provincial-park /cabot-beach

**Open year-round; campgrounds and facilities open from early June to late September**

&#9855; (Check ahead)

At the tip of Malpeque Bay sits the largest park in western Prince Edward Island. A broad swimming beach surrounded by red cliffs is the undisputed highlight of this park, which has great day-use facilities and a nice campground. Showers, bathrooms, picnic shelters, accessible playground equipment, a beach mat and a floating chair make it possible for everyone to enjoy a fun day at the beach.

The scenery is lovely, and you can enjoy wonderful views from the red cliffs surrounding the beach. Keep an eye out for birds in and around the park — Malpeque Bay is recognized as a globally significant Important Bird Area. A large number of shorebirds pass through the park during their spring and fall migrations. You might see semipalmated plovers, ruddy turnstones, double-crested cormorants, common terns, northern gannets, great blue herons, ospreys, red-eyed vireos, chickadees, swallows, sparrows, yellow warblers, a variety of gull species and many other birds inside the park.

There are two historic structures inside this park

— Fish Island Lighthouse and Fanning School. The historic lighthouse makes a great photo op. Originally located on Fish Island, the lighthouse was relocated to Cabot Beach in 1989, reassembled and restored. The Fanning School was moved to the park in 1993, from its original location in the nearby community of Malpeque. It was built in 1847 and named for Lieutenant Governor Edmund Fanning, who established the grammar school for the advancement and education of local children. According to local folklore, Lucy Maud Montgomery, author of *Anne of Green Gables*, attended the Fanning School in 1888, when she stayed nearby with her aunt Emily (Macneill) Montgomery. The schoolhouse was used in the 1998 television series *Emily of New Moon*, based on Montgomery's Emily novels.

Cabot Beach Provincial Park hosted thousands of boy scouts from around the nation at Canadian scout jamborees in 1977 and 2001. The park is popular with locals and visitors alike, and you'll find a great mix of both whenever you visit. During the annual Cabot Beach Senior Day in mid-August, there is live entertainment.

↑ The former Fish Island Lighthouse, now stationed at Cabot Beach, was more specifically a range light.

← The red hue of Cabot Beach's cliffs and sand is caused by their high iron-oxide content.

# Prince Edward Island National Park

by Debbie Olsen

**More than 50 kilometres of trails lead to woodlands, coastal wetlands, beaches and dunes**

## What Makes This Hot Spot Hot?

- Accessible beach activities are a highlight of this park.
- Green Gables Heritage Place showcases one of Canada's famous literary landmarks.
- The park protects nesting habitat for the endangered piping plover.

**Address:** Cavendish-North Rustico: 7591 Cawnpore Ln, North Rustico, PE
Brackley-Dalvay: 983 Gulf Shore Pkwy, Stanhope, PE
Greenwich: 59 Wild Rose Rd, Greenwich, PE
**GPS:** Cavendish-North Rustico: 46.49205; −63.37973
Brackley-Dalvay: 46.42192; −63.11088
Greenwich: 46.44473; −62.68179
**Tel.:** (902) 566-7050
**Website:** www.pc.gc.ca/en /pn-np/pe/pei-ipe/index

**Open year-round; facilities open June to early September**

&#9855; **(Check ahead)**

Towering sandstone cliffs, beautiful sandy beaches, delicate sand dunes, freshwater wetlands and salt marshes can all be found in Prince Edward Island's only national park. Located along 60 kilometres of the island's north shore, this national park is divided into three unique and beautiful sections: Cavendish-North Rustico, Brackley-Dalvay and Greenwich.

The park's supervised beaches are a real highlight for many visitors. Three of the beaches have accessibility features such as accessible washrooms, access ramps, buoyant beach wheelchairs and mobility mats that allow visitors with mobility challenges to fully enjoy a day at the shore.

A short distance from Cavendish Beach, you can find Green Gables Heritage Place, where you can spend an afternoon getting to know author Lucy Maud Montgomery's beloved *Anne of Green Gables*. Through interpretive exhibits at Green Gables Visitor Centre, you can learn about the life of the author, the characters she created and the Cavendish landscape that was the setting for her bestselling 1908 novel. Green Gables is part of L. M. Montgomery's

Cavendish National Historic Site, which includes the privately operated site of L. M. Montgomery's Cavendish Home. (Combination passes are available for purchase that allow admission to both sites.)

In 1998 the park was expanded to include 400 hectares of the Greenwich Peninsula, which contains rare U-shaped parabolic sand dunes. Archaeological digs in this region uncovered evidence of Paleo-Indigenous people dating back 10,000 years.

The park's diverse ecosystems support a variety of flora and fauna. More than 600 species of plants have been identified inside the park, including the provincial flower, the lady's slipper. Mammals to look for include red foxes, beavers, snowshoe hares, coyotes, minks, weasels and raccoons. In the waters just offshore, you might see seals, porpoises, dolphins and pilot and minke whales.

Birdwatching inside the park is excellent. The park is a designated Important Bird Area. It's possible to see the endangered piping plover, which nests inside the park. Other birds commonly seen include yellow warblers, belted kingfishers, grackles, gulls, sparrows, blue jays, red-winged blackbirds, great blue herons, bald eagles and ospreys.

Cycling and hiking are great ways to explore this coastal park. Paved two-way multi-purpose trails called Gulf Shore Way West (in Cavendish-North Rustico) and Gulf Shore Way East (in Brackley-Dalvay) provide wonderful views of the red sandstone Cavendish Cliffs, the Covehead Harbour Lighthouse, sand dunes, wetlands and beaches. A total of 14 hiking trails run through the park.

No matter how you choose to get around, you're sure to love all this national park has to offer.

↑ Boardwalks allow visitors to explore the parabolic dune system and wetlands that make up the Greenwich section of the park.

← The Stanhope Beach and Cavendish Beach areas of the park have both accessible beaches and campgrounds.

↓ The lady's slipper was named Prince Edward Island's official flower in 1947.

# Gros Morne National Park

by Debbie Olsen

**A remarkable landscape of mountains, valleys, fjords, cliffs, lakes, waterfalls, forests and beaches is found in this UNESCO World Heritage Site**

## What Makes This Hot Spot Hot?

- This park is famed for its outstanding and diverse scenic beauty.
- The diverse habitats in this park support a unique mixture of flora and fauna, from temperate and boreal species to Arctic species.
- Visitors can walk on the Earth's mantle and gain insight into the processes of continental drift.

**Address**: Rte 430, Rocky Harbour, NL
**GPS**: 49.57212; −57.87497
**Tel.**: (709) 458-2417
**Website**: www.pc.gc.ca/en /pn-np/nl/grosmorne/index

**Park open year-round; most facilities open mid-May to mid-October**

&#9855; (Check ahead)

This 1,805-square-kilometre park on the western coast of Newfoundland is dominated by two landscapes: an alpine landscape and a coastal lowland that borders the Gulf of St. Lawrence. The exceptional scenic beauty and diversity of this protected wilderness is part of the reason UNESCO designated it a World Heritage Site in 1987. The park's unique geology was the other major consideration. In the Tablelands region of the park, you can walk on the Earth's mantle, which is normally found far below the crust but was pushed up by powerful forces 500 million years ago. Exploring the geology of this park reveals fascinating information about plate tectonics and the processes of continental drift.

The park was named for Newfoundland's second-tallest mountain peak, which stands at 806 metres and is located inside its boundaries. The French name, *Mont Gros Morne*, literally means "big dreary mountain." It is part of the Long Range Mountains,

which are an outlying range of the Appalachians. These mountains were shaped by colliding continents and then reshaped by massive glaciers, which left sections of oceanic crust and part of the Earth's mantle exposed. This fascinating geology has contributed greatly to our understanding of geological evolution and the forces that shaped our planet.

Hiking is a great way to see some of the spectacular scenery in this park. There are more than 100 kilometres of trails that range in difficulty and length. You can join an organized interpretive group hike or venture out on your own on one of 20 different hiking trails.

For an equally scenic look at the park, experience a boat tour of Western Brook Pond or Trout River Pond. The Western Brook Pond tour provides a look from the bottom up at a spectacular glacier-carved land-locked fjord with tall waterfalls and ancient cliffs. The Trout River Pond tour lets you see the amazing geology of the Tablelands from a Zodiac boat and provides

access to a normally inaccessible area of the park.

The diverse habitat in this park allows for an equally diverse mixture of plants and animals, and you can find temperate, boreal and Arctic species here. Moose, woodland caribou, black bears, red foxes, Arctic foxes, snowshoe hares, lynx, otters and beavers make their home inside the park. In the summer, harbour seals and pilot, minke, fin and humpback whales can be seen in St. Paul's Inlet.

A wide variety of birds are spotted in every season, including species you wouldn't expect to find in the same park. Look for boreal chickadees, northern saw-whet owls, Canada jays and black-backed woodpeckers in the boreal forest. Along the coast, you can see seabirds like northern gannets, common eiders, plovers and common loons as well as bald eagles, goldeneyes and mergansers. In the Arctic-alpine habitat of the Long Range Mountains, you might see rock ptarmigans, white-crowned sparrows and American tree sparrows.

Gros Morne National Park is a wondrous place with dramatic scenery, fascinating geology, diverse wildlife and many activities for visitors to enjoy.

↑ A boat tour of Western Brook Pond is a memorable way to experience this iconic feature of Gros Morne.

↑↑ The Tablelands Trail leads visitors into this geologically fascinating area.

# Fogo Island and Change Islands

by Debbie Olsen

*Icebergs, seabirds and humpback whales drift past these islands off the coast of central Newfoundland*

## What Makes This Hot Spot Hot?

- The islands are steeped in history and maritime charm.
- Visitors can see species typical of the maritime Subarctic climate, such as puffins, caribou and foxes.
- Change Islands is home to a Newfoundland pony refuge.

**Address**: Fogo Island Visitor Centre: Hwy 333, 70 Man o' War Cove Rd, Fogo Island, NL
Change Islands Interpretation Centre: 12 km north of ferry terminal, Change Islands, NL
**GPS**:
Fogo Island: 49.58016; −54.28792
Change Islands:
49.66362; −54.40215
**Tel.**: Fogo Island: (709) 627-3570
Change Islands: (709) 621-3177
**Websites**:
www.townoffogoisland.ca
and www.changeislands.ca

**Open year-round;
visitor centres open
June to September**

&#9855; **(Limited, check ahead)**

Situated off the coast of central Newfoundland, these islands seem to be lost in time — a sort of Brigadoon, where most things haven't changed in decades. Fogo Island feels like the edge of the world, and there are some people who feel that it literally is: the Flat Earth Society identified Fogo Island's Brimstone Head as one of the four corners of the Earth. When you are standing at the top of this rocky outcrop in Brimstone Head Park gazing out at the seemingly endless expanse of the Atlantic Ocean, the description seems apt.

Fogo Island is the largest of the offshore islands in the province of Newfoundland and Labrador, and it is home to the internationally renowned Fogo Island Inn. Most people get to the island by ferry from the terminal at Farewell, but there are charter air options from Gander, Appleton and Twillingate.

Change Islands can only be reached by sea and are connected to Fogo Island and mainland Newfoundland by ferry. It's a 25-minute ferry ride from Farewell to Change Islands and a 50-minute ride from Farewell to Fogo.

If the islands' rugged, wind-swept landscapes don't win you over, the friendly islanders undoubtedly will. The islands are home to 12 small communities that have become artists' havens. You can walk through fishing villages filled with brightly coloured clapboard houses, lush gardens and old fishing sheds. These islands are places where people go to bed with the doors unlocked and take life at a slower pace.

One of the best ways to get to know the geology, flora and fauna of the islands is on the hiking trails and walking paths. As you walk, keep an eye out for whales and seabirds in the waters offshore. Puffins, razorbills, dovekies, evening grosbeaks, king eiders, harlequin ducks, white-winged scoters and gannets are just a few of the birds you might see. Little Fogo Island is a significant nesting site for Atlantic puffins. You might also see land mammals like caribou, coyotes, beavers and foxes. Caribou were introduced

to Fogo Island in the mid-20th century, and some migrated to Change Islands.

Change Islands are also home to a Newfoundland pony refuge that is dedicated to the preservation of this unique breed. There was a time when almost every household in the province had one of these sturdy ponies, but things changed with the advent of mechanization, and the species was brought to the brink of extinction.

In this corner of the Earth, you'll discover a place where time moves slower and where locals mark island life with seven seasons instead of four: winter, pack ice, spring, trap berth, summer, berry-picking and temperamental late fall. There's no other place like it.

↑ Caribou populations on Fogo Island have seen decline, but biologists think the population numbers are now showing signs of improvement.

↖ Hiking paths around Fogo Island take visitors over rugged terrain, and springtime hikers can expect to see millennia-old icebergs floating by in the ocean.

# Akami-Uapishk<sup>U</sup>-KakKasuak-Mealy Mountains National Park Reserve

by Debbie Olsen

**Labrador's newest national park protects a pristine landscape of mountains, tundra, coasts, forests, islands and rivers**

## What Makes This Hot Spot Hot?

- The landscape that surrounds the Mealy Mountains is filled with wild rivers, waterfalls and numerous boreal animal species.
- The park protects cultural landscapes of importance to Indigenous Peoples.
- Much of the range of the Mealy Mountains' threatened caribou herd is protected in this national park.

**Address**: There is no direct road access into the park; to fly in, make arrangements with outfitters or air charter companies
**GPS**: 53.57226; −58.34769
**Tel.**: (709) 896-2394
**Website**: www.pc.gc.ca/en/pn-np/nl/mealy/index

**Open year-round**

The Mealy Mountains are at the heart of this national park reserve in Labrador. In fact, the word "mountain" is used three times in the name of the park: *Akami-Uapishk<sup>U</sup>* is derived from an Innu word that means "white mountains across," and *KakKasuak* is a Labrador Inuit word that means "mountain." Rising up to 1,180 metres, these glacier-carved mountains tower over Lake Melville and several inland fjords. It's a place that is beautiful and remote — a place with no roads.

The idea of making the Mealy Mountains a national park was discussed decades ago, but in 2017 it became a reality, when 10,700 square kilometres of land on the east side of Labrador was incorporated into a new national park. Visitors to this park must be self-reliant, well equipped and take precautions to ensure they are safe in this wild place that is home to wolves, black bears and, on occasion, polar bears. With minimal infrastructure and services, including search-and-rescue capabilities, careful trip planning is essential.

This park is in the East Coast boreal natural region, and as such it protects many boreal forest animal species. The threatened Mealy Mountains' herd of woodland caribou, wolves, martens, black bears and two species of foxes are commonly found here as well as many different bird species.

One of the scenic highlights of the park is a place on the coast of the Labrador Sea called the Wunderstrands. It is an extensive 50-kilometre-long stretch of sandy beach that is one of the

↑ **Visitors will feel at one with nature in this vast and remote national park reserve.**

icons of the park and has a fascinating and long history with Indigenous Peoples. Viking explorers named it the Wunderstrands when they sailed the region. It can be explored by kayak or boat from Cartwright or Rigolet.

This remote park is not easy to get to. It takes effort and planning, but it's a place that protects a vast amount of unique and pristine habitat that has long been important to Indigenous Peoples.

↑ **The threatened Mealy Mountains caribou herd roam the area, and the establishment of the park reserve will help protect some of their key habitats.**

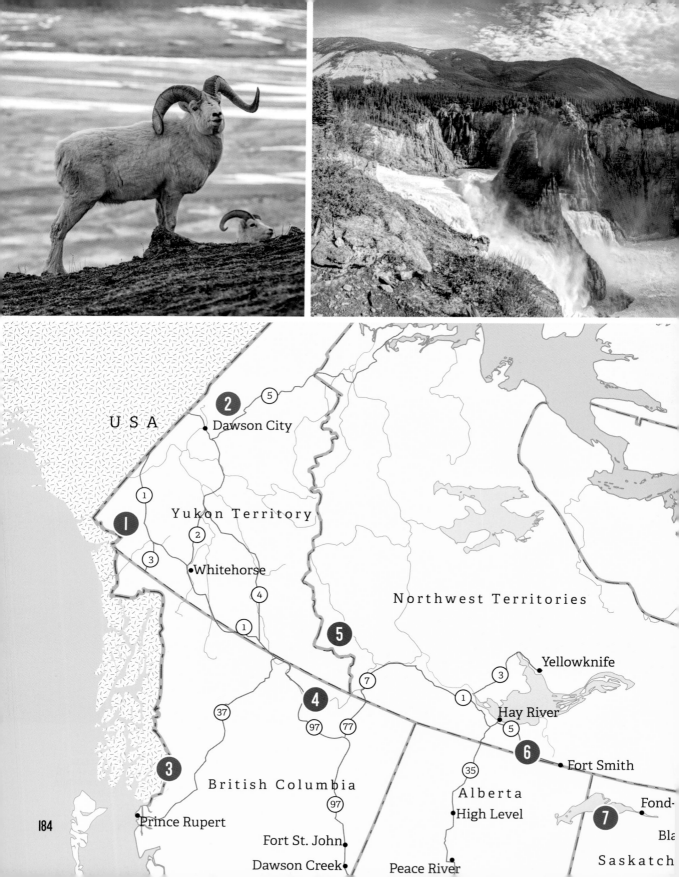

USA

2 ⑤

• Dawson City

① Yukon Territory

1

② 

③

•Whitehorse

④

Northwest Territories

①

5

⑦

③

Yellowknife

4

Hay River

37

⑨⑦ ⑦⑦

⑤

6

Fort Smith

3

British Columbia

35

Alberta

High Level

⑨⑦

Fond-

7

Bla

Saskatch

184

•Prince Rupert

Fort St. John•

Dawson Creek•

Peace River•

# The North

# Kluane National Park and Reserve

by Debbie Olsen

*Kluane is part of a UNESCO World Heritage Site that is the largest internationally protected area in the world*

## What Makes This Hot Spot Hot?

- Kluane has both the tallest and largest mountains in Canada.
- Many large mammal species are found here, including North America's most genetically diverse grizzly bear population.
- The park hosts stunning wilderness scenery, including the largest non-polar icefield in the world.

**Address**: 280 Alaska Hwy (Hwy 1), Haines Junction, YT
**GPS**: 60.76245; –137.51427
**Tel.**: (867) 634-7207 (seasonal visitor centre); (867) 634-7250 (administrative office)
**Website**: www.pc.gc.ca/en /pn-np/yt/kluane/index

**Open year-round; the visitor centre is open mid-May to mid-September**

&#9855; **(Check ahead)**

"Larger than life" might be a cliché, but it's a phrase that fits Kluane National Park. Massive mountains and glaciers dominate the landscape. Kluane is home to 17 of the country's 20 tallest mountains, and the world's largest non-polar icefield, which permanently covers more than half of the 21,980-square-kilometre park. Among the colossal peaks stands Mount Logan, Canada's highest mountain and the second-tallest mountain in North America.

The forests and tundra that surround the St. Elias Mountains teem with life. Kluane has an incredible diversity of plant life — more than 200 species of plants can be found in the green belt region, and this diversity of flora provides habitat for many species of birds and mammals.

More than 150 species of birds have been seen in the park, with 118 species known to nest here — including birds of prey like American kestrels, northern harriers, bald eagles and golden eagles. Canada jays, black-capped chickadees, boreal chickadees and willow ptarmigans can be spotted year-round.

Kluane's green belt also provides habitat for many mammal species. Dall sheep are by far the most plentiful large land mammals in the park. These wild sheep are slightly smaller than bighorn sheep and have thinner horns that flare outward from their faces. There are also large numbers of moose and mountain goats. Wolves, coyotes, foxes, martens, wolverines and lynx roam the park along with black bears and grizzly bears.

DNA testing on the grizzly bear population revealed that this park has one of the most genetically diverse populations in the world. This is important because genetic diversity helps maintain the health of a species and allows for better adaptation

to environmental changes. Grizzly bear populations have been declining throughout North America, and this has resulted in declining genetic diversity in many populations.

There are no roads inside the park, but the Haines and Alaska Highways (Highways 3 and 1, respectively) run along the northeastern edge. There are several access points where you can hike to lakes, enjoy a picnic or camp.

Several companies offer "flight-seeing" trips in small planes from Haines Junction, Burwash or Kluane Lake that allow you to get a closer view of the interior of the park, the stunning mountains and massive icefield, which incorporates glaciers that stretch for 60 kilometres. Depending on weather conditions, planes might land on a glacier and allow passengers to get out and explore.

At Haines Junction, you'll find a large building that houses the Parks Canada and Yukon visitor centres as well as the Da Ku Cultural Centre, which focuses on the history and culture of the local Indigenous Peoples. Kluane National Park and Reserve lies within the traditional territory of the Southern Tutchone People, who established trails through this wilderness that have been used for centuries. Today the park is cooperatively managed by Kluane First Nation, Champagne and Aishihik First Nations and Parks Canada.

↑ A "flight-seeing" trip over Kluane National Park is a great way to take in the rugged beauty of this remote wilderness.

↓ Dall sheep are often spotted on Thechàl Dhâl (Sheep Mountain), and the southeast face of the mountain is an important winter foraging area that's protected.

# Tombstone Territorial Park

by Debbie Olsen

*This territorial park encompasses over 2,200 square kilometres of geologically unique and ecologically diverse wilderness*

## What Makes This Hot Spot Hot?

- Visitors will discover scenic views of rugged mountains, Arctic tundra and permafrost landforms.
- The park is filled with diverse flora and fauna.
- Numerous hiking trails can be easily accessed from the Dempster Highway.

**Address**: Dempster Hwy (Hwy 5) at km 71.5, north of Dawson City, YT
**GPS**: 64.50294; −138.21977
**Tel.**: (867) 993-7714
**Website**: www.yukon.ca/en /tombstone-territorial-park

Open year-round; Tombstone Interpretive Centre is open from late May to September

↗ **Hoary marmots here hibernate from September to April and live in colonies of up to 11 members.**

Just south of the Arctic Circle, Tombstone Territorial Park is everything you imagine the Yukon to be. It's so scenically beautiful and diverse that it has been called the "Patagonia of the North." In the south end of the park, about 112 kilometres outside Dawson City, you'll find mountains, forests and river valleys — including Tombstone Mountain, for which the park is named. At the north end, you'll find treeless tundra and unusual permafrost landforms like pingos and palsas.

This wide variety of landscapes provides habitat for a diverse array of birds, mammals, plants and insects. The region is home to the Tr'ondëk Hwëch'in First Nation, who have hunted, camped and traded here for thousands of years. The park is co-operatively managed by the Yukon territorial government and the Tr'ondëk Hwëch'in First Nation.

Birders have spotted more than 150 species inside the park and confirmed 42 breeding species. Some of the most sought-after bird sightings include surfbirds, northern wheatears, Smith's longspurs, long-tailed jaegers, wandering tattlers, gyrfalcons, golden eagles, harlequin ducks and

northern hawk owls. Willow, rock and white-tailed ptarmigans are all present in the park. If you spot all three in one trip, you've achieved what the Yukon Bird Club calls a Ptarmigan Grand Slam.

A wide variety of mammals are also found here. Dall sheep, caribou, moose, grizzly and black bears, wolves, hoary marmots, pikas, shrews and voles inhabit Tombstone Territorial Park.

The Dempster Highway bisects the park, and park services are located along the highway corridor, including an interpretive centre with displays, information and interpretive programs — including scheduled guided day hikes of Grizzly Trail. There is one front-country campground and three designated backcountry

campgrounds: Grizzly, Divide and Talus Lakes. If you plan to stay in backcountry areas, please visit the park's website to book backcountry campsites for your requested dates.

Tombstone Outfitters offers guided horseback rides in Tombstone Territorial Park. Hourly, daily and overnight trips into the backcountry can be arranged. They also offer guided hunting expeditions on horseback.

Be aware that Tombstone is remote and rugged. Visitors should be prepared for rough terrain and drastic weather changes — even on day hikes. There is no food, gas, cellphone or Wi-Fi service inside the park. Make sure your gas tank is full and your four-wheel-drive vehicle is in good working order before you set out on the Dempster Highway.

↑ Tombstone Territorial Park can be experienced on foot, by car or by horse.

↓ This territorial park is a wilderness hiker's haven, with challenging terrain and spectacular scenery.

# Bear and Salmon Glaciers

by Lyndsay Fraser

*The glaciers are all on BC soil, but you will need your passport to make the most of these breathtaking views*

## What Makes This Hot Spot Hot?

- Views of beautiful glaciers and waterfalls are all along the drive into Stewart.
- Salmon Glacier is the fifth-largest glacier in Canada.
- Marmots and other wildlife can be seen from the road and lookouts.

**Address:** Glacier Hwy (Stewart Hwy or Hwy 37A), between Meziadin Junction and Stewart, BC
**GPS:** 56.097455; −129.667406
**Tel.:** (250) 636-9224 (Stewart Visitor Centre)
**Websites:** www.env.gov.bc.ca /bcparks/explore/parkpgs /bear_gl and www.stewart cassiarhighway.com /attractions/salmon-glacier

**Open year-round, conditions permitting**

The drive along the appropriately named Glacier Highway (also known as Stewart Highway and Highway 37A) into the small town of Stewart is one of the most picturesque drives in British Columbia, with spectacular views around every corner. There are many pull-offs along the road to support the nature lover's desire to stop and admire the dramatic surroundings, as the drive takes you past many glaciers, mountain waterfalls, rushing rivers, rolling streams and steep rock walls. Watch for wildlife on the road, as black bears and grizzlies are found in the area, and there are often opportunities for roadside birding. Listen for the short, burry calls of the western tanager for a chance to catch a glimpse of this shy yet lavishly coloured bird.

Glaciers often appear blue simply because, just as in large bodies of water, the molecules in these massive pieces of compressed ice absorb other colours of light more efficiently. The pressure that creates such a dense piece of ice also squeezes out air bubbles that would otherwise make the ice appear white.

The most famous ice formation along this stretch of highway is the Bear Glacier, protected within provincial parkland. Although it once completely filled the Bear River Pass, the glacier began to retreat in the 1940s, and where once was ice, now a lake has formed. Although the beautiful glacial tongue is still an awe-inspiring roadside stop, it is worth looking for evidence in the rocks and slopes of its once grander size. This rapidly shrinking glacier is a startling reminder that glacial retreats are among the most dramatic indicators of climate change.

Bring your passport with you on this trip, since once in Stewart, a worthwhile crossing to American soil and back across the border into BC will bring you to the magnificent Salmon Glacier. The drive takes you through the Alaskan ghost town of Hyder, where the only customs you will encounter is when you re-enter Canada. The 37-kilometre drive to the lookout over

the glacier provides additional wildlife viewing opportunities. You will have a good chance of seeing hoary marmots along the way between May and August, the only months of the year they are not hibernating. Marmots thrive in rocky alpine terrain, hiding from predators in burrows. In the summer you may see moms feeding and sunbathing with their babies, who stay with them for two years before venturing off on their own.

Salmon Glacier, found just on the Canadian side of the border, is the fifth-largest glacier in the country. From the viewpoint you can see where the enormous icefield splits into two tongues. Look for terminal moraines near the glacial toe, where sediments scraped and carried by the river of ice are deposited.

↑ Views of the massive Salmon Glacier are worth the trek across American soil.

↖ Meltwater rushes down from the toe of Bear Glacier.

# Liard River Hot Springs Provincial Park

by Lyndsay Fraser

**Exceptional and provincially unique organisms call these hot waters home**

## What Makes This Hot Spot Hot?

- This is the only place in the world where you can find hotwater physa snails.
- Species found way outside their normal range thrive in the warm waters here.
- Wood bison are abundant within the park and easy to spot from the road.

**Address:** Alaska Hwy (Hwy 97) at km 765, about 60 km north of Muncho Lake Provincial Park
**GPS:** 59.419877; –126.089826
**Tel.:** (250) 776-7000
**Website:** www.env.gov.bc.ca /bcparks/explore/parkpgs /liard_rv_hs

**Open year-round**

&#9855; **(Check ahead)**

Like many hot springs scattered across British Columbia, Liard River Hot Springs Provincial Park is a popular destination for those looking for a tranquil and steaming dip in natural waters. However, these springs are unlike any other in the province and are home to species found nowhere else in the world. As a general rule, hot springs are brimming with specialized organisms that are able to live in these unusual and harsh conditions. These hot springs take it one step further, providing refuge to some rare species, even by hot spring standards.

The Liard River system has at least six hot springs feeding into pools and streams that eventually drain into a marsh. As hot water flows into shallower areas farther from the source, it cools off, depositing calcium carbonate that was picked up as the water moved through underground limestone deposits.

The carbonate minerals from the water harden to form deposits of tufa, a type of limestone. Chara, thought to be a late common ancestor of algae and land plants, becomes encrusted in the calcium carbonate and provides a habitat for Liard River's rarest animals.

The hotwater physa is a tiny freshwater snail found here and nowhere else in the world. The snails thrive in waters between 23°C and 40°C, feeding on organisms that live on the chara's crusty surface. Between 3 and 9 millimetres in length, this tiny mollusc needs the support of the park's visitors to ensure its survival, or else it faces global extinction. Do not disturb the sensitive habitat in the marsh, as the wide boardwalk provides fabulous viewing opportunities in this unique environment without having to touch anything. The use of all soaps, oils, sunscreens and other skin products by bathers

is prohibited in the springs upstream to protect this spectacular nature hot spot.

Other provincially rare natives to the marsh are thankfully much easier to spot than the miniscule physas. A population of lake chub is found here, able to tolerate the high temperatures. Look for this small, well-camouflaged fish darting around in small clearings in the marshy water surrounding the boardwalk. The plains forktail, a dainty damselfly typically found in the most southern reaches of Canada's prairies, can be spotted along the boardwalk. Unique populations like these are probably relicts of warmer days: During a warming after the retreat of the glaciers that once covered British Columbia, these species were likely more widespread, but their range is now constrained to the hot springs.

Liard River Hot Springs Provincial Park is also home to some impressive large mammals, including moose, which are sometimes seen visiting the warm marsh waters. In the forests surrounding the hot springs, the Nahanni population of wood bison is locally abundant. Watch for the hefty solitary males, who may weigh up to 900 kilograms, feeding or resting in clearings beside the highway as well as large herds of females and their calves, often accompanied by yearlings and a few bulls. As North America's largest land mammal, wood bison are hard to miss, and these imposing giants are certainly not shy, requiring traffic to yield to them and not vice versa.

↑ A raised boardwalk takes you up to the Hanging Garden, where tufa creates a terraced base for plants to grow.

↓ A wood bison calf makes for a memorable wildlife sighting in this provincial park.

# Nahanni National Park Reserve

by Debbie Olsen

**This UNESCO-designated wilderness park is a true bucket-list destination for adventurers**

## What Makes This Hot Spot Hot?

- This remote park reserve hosts one of the most spectacular wild rivers in North America.
- Visitors can see Canada's greatest wilderness waterfall — which is double the height of Niagara Falls.
- Climbers and hikers can discover incredible scenery in the Cirque of the Unclimbables.

**Address**: There is no direct road access into the park. To fly in, make arrangements with outfitters or air charter companies
**GPS**: 61.48088; –125.52471
**Tel.**: (867) 695-7750
**Website**: www.pc.gc.ca/en/pn-np/nt/nahanni/index

**Open year-round**

Over many centuries, the South Nahanni River has carved some of the deepest canyons in Canada through a 30,000-square-kilometre wilderness filled with sheer granite peaks and other remarkable geological landforms. The South Nahanni is one of Canada's most epic heritage rivers, and it is the heart of a legendary national park and UNESCO World Heritage Site.

This wild land has been the home of the Dene People for thousands of years, and they call it Nahʔą Dehé, which means "river of the land of the Nahʔą People." Today the Dehcho First Nations welcome adventurers to their homeland.

There are no roads leading into Nahanni National Park Reserve. Paddling is the traditional mode of transportation, and the South Nahanni River is on the wish list of many adventurers. It is highly recommended that those who paddle here do so with a registered, licenced outfitter.

Canoers and kayakers have died while travelling on the South Nahanni, the Flat and Little Nahanni Rivers. Even the most experienced paddlers and hikers can find themselves in the wrong place at the wrong time. Nahanni National Park Reserve is a remote and at times unforgiving place. Travellers need to be informed, well-equipped and experienced to deal with weather, wildfire and river hazards, including flash floods.

The park can also be accessed via float plane from Fort Simpson, Fort Liard and Muncho Lake (in northern British Columbia). Hikers often access the park this way. It's also possible to take a day trip or a "flight-seeing" trip that gives an overview of some of the most beautiful areas of the park, including Virginia Falls, Ram Plateau, Ram River Canyons, Glacier Lake, Nahanni Karstlands, the Ragged Mountain Range and Gahnhthah (Rabbitkettle) mineral springs, home to Canada's largest tufa mound. Tufa mounds are limestone rock formations created by the precipitation of dissolved minerals, predominantly calcium carbonate, from thermal

spring water. The North Mound is 30 metres high and 60 metres wide, and it is estimated to be 10,000 years old. It can only be accessed on guided hikes with park staff.

Of all the sights in Nahanni National Park Reserve, the 96-metre Virginia Falls is not to be missed. These breathtaking falls are double the height of Niagara Falls and widely considered to be Canada's most stunning wild waterfall. They are bisected by a rock formation known as Mason's Rock. A fortunate few have seen these thundering falls and felt their mist.

For climbers, the Cirque of the Unclimbables is a dreamlike landscape filled with sheer granite peaks that seem to defy gravity. Classic climbs include Lotus Flower Tower, Mount Proboscis and Middle Huey Spire. But you don't have to climb to enjoy this area of the park. Hiking through this landscape and camping in the Fairy Meadow is the adventure of a lifetime for an experienced outdoorsperson.

Nahʔą Dehé is an incomparable wilderness and an epic journey for paddlers, climbers and hikers who wish to connect with a rugged landscape and the people who call it home.

↑ Twice the height of Niagara Falls, Virginia Falls is arguably one of the most beautiful falls in Canada and can be accessed by floatplane through a licensed outfitter.

↖ Visitors can walk on tufa mounds on guided hikes.

# Wood Buffalo National Park

by Debbie Olsen

**Canada's largest national park is a UNESCO World Heritage Site and contains one of the world's largest inland deltas**

## What Makes This Hot Spot Hot?

- Wood Buffalo is home to the world's largest population of free-roaming wood bison.
- The area contains the last remaining natural nesting area of the endangered whooping crane.
- The park is the world's largest dark sky preserve.

**Address:**
Fort Smith: 149 MacDougal Rd, Fort Smith, NT
Fort Chipewyan: 124B Mackenzie Ave, Fort Chipewyan, AB
**GPS:**
Fort Smith: 60.00576; −111.87748
Fort Chipewyan:
58.71363; −111.15149
**Tel.:** (867) 872-7960
**Website:** www.pc.gc.ca/en/pn-np/nt/woodbuffalo/index

**Open year-round; hours for visitor centres vary depending on season**

Canada's largest national park spans 44,807 square kilometres in northeastern Alberta and south-central Northwest Territories. Established in 1922, it is the second-largest national park in the world. To put it in perspective, the park is a bit larger than Switzerland.

Wood Buffalo was declared a UNESCO World Heritage Site in 1983, in part for the biological diversity of the Peace-Athabasca Delta, one of the world's largest freshwater deltas. Among the many ecosystems within the park are some of the largest undisturbed grass and sedge meadows left in North America.

The world's largest herd of free-roaming wood bison are also found here, and it's the only place where the predator-prey relationship between wolves and bison has continued, unbroken, for centuries.

In addition to the bison for which the area is most famous, many species of wildlife are found in the park's varied ecosystems. Bears, wolves, moose, lynx, martens, wolverines, foxes, beavers and snowshoe hares are a few of the wild mammal species found here. The park hosts the

world's largest beaver dam, and this 850-metre-long dam is so big it can be seen from space. The park also protects the only wild nesting area of the endangered whooping crane as well as some nesting sites of the threatened peregrine falcon. Note, however, that there is no public access to these nesting areas.

The prime area for birding is the Peace-Athabasca Delta. During the spring and fall, millions of migratory birds from all four North American flyways pass through the delta. Snow geese, sandhill cranes, hawks, eagles and owls are often seen.

The main office for this park is located in Fort Smith, Northwest Territories, with a satellite office located in Fort Chipewyan, Alberta. Fort Smith can be accessed year-round via paved roads, but the only way to reach Fort Chipewyan in the summer is by boat or plane. A winter ice road connects Fort Smith with Fort Chipewyan and Fort McMurray for about three months each year.

The payoff for the remoteness of this place is not only its wildness but also its night sky. Wood Buffalo National Park is the world's largest dark sky preserve. Here, constellations come to life and aurora viewing can be spectacular. The annual Dark Sky Festival in mid-August is a good time to visit if you're interested in stargazing.

**↑ The park encompasses diverse habitats, from forest to prairie to scenic wetlands and lakes.**

**← This wood bison is a member of the world's largest free-roaming wood bison herd.**

# Athabasca Sand Dunes Provincial Park

by Jenn Smith Nelson

*Boreal forest meets desert-like sand dunes to form one of Canada's most unlikely and unique landscapes*

## What Makes This Hot Spot Hot?

- This is the world's most northerly sand dune formation.
- The park is home to rare and endemic plant species.
- Lake Athabasca is the largest lake in Saskatchewan and the 20th-largest lake in the world.

**Address**: There is no direct road access into the park. To fly in, make arrangements with outfitters or air charter companies
**GPS**: 59.04684; –108.8236
**Tel.**: (800) 205-7070
**Website**: www.tourism saskatchewan.com/places-to-go

**Open year-round; wilderness camping is available May long weekend to Labour Day; park is non-operational with no facilities**

Mountains of sand flowing out of the boreal forest make the Athabasca Sand Dunes one of the most unique and unexpected land features in Canada. As a pack in–pack out destination with no facilities, services or roads into it, it's not the easiest place to visit. However, for good reasons, it tops many trip wish lists.

This fragile environment, protected by the creation of the Athabasca Sand Dunes Provincial Park in 1992, is truly exceptional. Found in an ultra-remote expanse in northwestern Saskatchewan, these 30,000 hectares of sandy wilderness encompass the largest set of active sand dunes in Canada and are the most northerly sand surface on the planet.

The dunes started life as a delta in a large freshwater lake. The delta was formed when glaciers melted and deposited huge amounts of sand and silt into Lake Athabasca. Over time, the lake's water levels dropped, revealing massive sand deposits. Some of the wind-sculpted ridges and hills tower over 30 metres in height.

For an area covered in sand, the diversity of plant life is surprising. Flora thrives thanks to the subarctic forest's rock-bound soil, which provides ideal conditions for plants' root systems to spread. There are over 300 plant species in the park, of which 50 are considered rare and 10 are endemic, in other words, not found anywhere else in the world. The large-headed woolly yarrow, felt-leaf willow, Athabasca thrift, Mackenzie hairgrass and sand stitchwort are a few of the endemics. The rarest is the impoverished pinweed, a plant with multiple stems that extend outward from a single taproot.

The dunes are home to several mammals, such as moose, wolves, bears, martens and caribou. It's also a birdwatching mecca — 30 species of wood warblers have been spotted here.

Lake Athabasca is noteworthy as well. At 7,850 square kilometres and with a maximum depth of 124 metres, it's the largest lake in Saskatchewan and the 20th-largest lake in the world.

Access to the park is by float plane or boat. The park is recommended for visitors with wilderness experience, though guided tours are available. The best time to visit is between June and August.

You must check in with a conservation officer prior to visiting. As the park and its ecosystem are delicate, visitors are urged to avoid exploring or camping in off-limit areas, such as on the desert pavement, which is a layer of worn pebbles that sits atop the sands, appearing as a walkway through the dunes. Please only set up in one of the six designated primitive campsites.

↑ Mackenzie hairgrass is one of 10 endemic plant species found in the park.

↖ It's no mirage — in this provincial park, an unlikely pairing of water and desert-like sand dunes occurs.

↤ The massive dunes cover over 30,000 hectares.

# Churchill

by Doug O'Neill

**Known as the "Polar Bear Capital of the World," Churchill is the go-to destination not just for polar bear viewing but also to see beloved belugas and the northern lights**

## What Makes This Hot Spot Hot?

- Churchill is the most popular human settlement in the world to view the majestic polar bear up close.
- About 60,000 beluga whales congregate along the Hudson Bay coast from June to September.
- Churchill's position directly beneath the northern hemisphere's auroral oval makes it one of the best locations on the planet to witness the northern lights.

**Address**: There is no direct road access into Churchill. Flights from Winnipeg via Gimli are popular. Trains are available between Winnipeg and Churchill
**GPS**: 58.76841; −94.16496
**Tel.**: (800) 665-0040
**Website**: www.everythingchurchill.com

**Open year-round**

&#9855; (Limited, check ahead)

Mention "Churchill" to a nature lover, and you'll get at least one of three responses: polar bears, beluga whales or the northern lights.

While polar bears put Churchill on the map (it's recognized as the "Polar Bear Capital of the World"), most people visit this region on the southern edge of Canada's Arctic to fulfill a bucket-list dream that also includes up-close encounters with beluga whales and witnessing the aurora borealis. The time of year you decide to visit will likely be dictated by what you wish to observe.

Churchill, long categorized as "the accessible Arctic," is home to wildlife species that are native to three distinct ecozones: Arctic marine, Arctic tundra and boreal forest.

Three options are available to observe the polar bears: safely seated in a tundra buggy, eye-to-eye through strong buffalo fences that surround a handful of northern lodges or on foot with an expert guide on a walking safari. The prime viewing times are in October and November, when the polar bears travel from their summer habitat on the tundra back to their ice-and-snow-covered seal-hunting territory on the Hudson Bay. However, many bears come as early as July.

Then there are other wildlife enthusiasts who are besotted with beluga whales, which have been called "sea canaries" because of their singular high-pitched whistles, chirps, clicks and eerie calls from below the water. From June to September, about 60,000 belugas (the largest concentration of the species in the world) take over the waters off the Hudson Bay coastline, where they seem comfortable with the kayaks, Zodiacs and tour boats that enable visitors to watch them (some of them 3 to 4 metres in length) frolic in the water.

The region has lots of other flora and fauna to discover — Arctic foxes, red foxes, moose, black bears, caribou, wolves, seals, 250 species of birds (migratory and shorebirds) and more than 400 native plant species, including scarlet bearberries, yellow willows and white mountain avens.

There is also one of the planet's greatest celestial spectacles. Do the northern lights — that colourful, sweeping, dancing explosion of light in the northern night sky — actually make a sound? It's an oft-debated discussion among night-sky watchers.

Some claim there's a swishing sound while others talk about a crackling noise when the lights appear. What is 100 per cent certain, however, is the astounding beauty of this phenomenon, which occurs when charged particles from the sun become trapped in the Earth's

↑ Visitors on board a tundra buggy can safely encounter polar bears in their natural setting.

↖ The Churchill region is one of the world's biggest polar bear denning areas, so mothers and cubs are frequently spotted.

magnetic field, resulting in a vibrant display of greens, purples, reds and yellows across the dark northern skies. The best times to view the aurora borealis? On a clear night between January and March and from late August or early September to December. (The aurora is typically not visible during May, June and July, when the nighttime skies tend to be bright.)

Nature enthusiasts can sign up for courses at the Churchill Northern Studies Centre, an independent not-for-profit research and education facility that offers a range of educational programming for students and visiting researchers. The centre, which also provides accommodation, is located 23 kilometres east of town.

After an extended disruption in rail service to Churchill, the Hudson Bay Railway line has been repaired, and Via Rail is operating regular services. It is always best to check ahead and book any tours and accommodations in advance.

↑ About 60,000 belugas (the largest concentration of the whales in the world) take over the waters off the Hudson Bay coastline from June to September.

↖ The red fox is one of many wildlife species that call the Churchill area home.

← Mountain white avens add a splash of colour to the Arctic landscape.

→ The optimal time to see the northern lights is on a clear night between January and March and from late August or early September to December.

# Auyuittuq National Park

by Debbie Olsen

**Located on Baffin Island, Auyuittuq is Canada's first national park north of the Arctic Circle**

## What Makes This Hot Spot Hot?

- Auyuittuq is home to Mount Thor, the Earth's highest sheer cliff.
- The park's coastal waters are teeming with wildlife, including polar bears, seals and narwhals.
- Parks Canada offers unique programming and guided excursions, including day trips to the Arctic Circle.

**Address**: There is no direct road access into the park. To access it by boat, make arrangements with outfitters in Pangnirtung or Qikiqtarjuaq
**GPS**: 67.55878; −64.02394
**Tel.**: (867) 473-2500 (Pangnirtung); (867) 927-8834 (Qikiqtarjuaq)
**Website**: www.pc.gc.ca/en /pn-np/nu/auyuittuq/index

**Open year-round**

Life is challenging in the harsh Arctic environment of Auyuittuq National Park, but that's what makes it so beautiful and such a special place to visit. More than a quarter of Nunavut's most accessible park is permanently covered in snow and ice. The Inuit named the area Auyuittuq, which means "the land that never melts."

Auyuittuq is incredibly diverse. Rugged granite peaks, glaciers, icefields, deep fjords, winding meltwater streams, rushing rivers and flat tundra make this one of Canada's most scenic national parks. Although vegetation is generally sparse, in summer there is a brief period when wildflowers like white mountain avens, yellow Arctic poppy, campion and purple saxifrage dot the tundra meadows.

Arctic hares, lemmings and a few barren-ground caribou survive inside the park's 19,500 square kilometres, hunted by wolves, Arctic foxes and weasels. The coast provides habitat for millions of seabirds, and coastal waters teem with life. Polar bears, walruses, ringed seals, belugas and narwhals hunt for fish in the icy Arctic waters.

At over 1,500 metres, Mount Thor is the Earth's tallest sheer cliff, and it's on the bucket-list of many experienced climbers. Mount Asgard's twin peaks (2,015 metres) are another climbing hot spot that was made famous in the parachute scene of the 1977 James Bond film *The Spy Who Loved Me*.

The peak travel months in the park are April, July and August. In summer, you can hike across the Arctic Circle on a 97-kilometre trek through Akshayuk Pass. In April you can do the same trip on skis, snowshoes or a snowmobile.

Parks Canada offers unique programming in Auyuittuq, including guided snowmobile day trips to the Arctic Circle and guided hiking trips to Ulu Peak. Both journeys give visitors the opportunity to interact with Inuit interpreters who share stories about the land, wildlife and people. You must register well in advance for these programs, and give yourself extra travel

time in case of flight delays due to inclement weather.

Canada's Far North is an unpredictable place that presents many challenges for travellers. Weather is variable and whiteout conditions can happen at any time of year. Advance planning and preparation is key to a successful journey into Auyuittuq. Visitors should familiarize themselves with the 28-page Parks Canada information guide and the polar bear safety pamphlet. All visitors must register in advance for a mandatory three-hour orientation session, and all trips into the park must be registered prior to entering and deregistered upon exiting. If you're travelling on your own, it's a good idea to hire a local guide or a polar bear guard.

Auyuittuq National Park is a special place that a fortunate few experience. To gain the most from your trip, be sure to take the time to get to know the local Inuit, who have lived on this land for thousands of years.

↑ **Mount Thor, Earth's tallest sheer cliff, stands out even in Auyuittuq's mountainous landscape.**

# Special Interest

# Best Multi-Day Backpacking Trails

↑ **Tsusiat Falls is one of the scenic stops along the West Coast Trail.**

You could say that trails are part of the fabric and culture of Canada. The Great Trail (formerly called the Trans-Canada Trail) stretches across the country and is the longest recreational trail in the world. But it's not the only exceptional trail in the nation. The country is criss-crossed with thousands of stunning pathways, including some of the best multi-day backpacking trails on the planet. The most popular backpacking trails must be reserved a full year in advance, and even when reservations are not required, advance planning and preparation are essential to a successful backpacking trip.

## West Coast Trail, BC

In British Columbia's Pacific Rim National Park Reserve, the 75-kilometre West Coast Trail (WCT) is a bucket-list hike. Over three to seven days, hikers ascend more than 100 ladders, wade through rivers, ride a ferry, cross bridges and walk across logs suspended over deep ravines to complete this challenging expedition. Scenery surrounding the trail includes gorgeous beaches, old-growth forests, a lighthouse and beautiful waterfalls. Hikers often see whales and other sea life along the way, and a tide table is absolutely essential when hiking here. Parks Canada maintains and operates the trail in cooperation with local Indigenous groups, and you have to reserve early if you want to hike it between May and September, when it's open.

## Chilkoot Trail
## National Historic Site,
## BC/Alaska (USA)

In some ways, a hike along the 53-kilometre Chilkoot Trail is a journey through time. Originally used as a trading route by the coastal Tlingit People, it became the primary passageway for thousands of prospectors and fortune seekers to reach the Yukon during the Klondike gold rush. It's a beautiful and extremely challenging hike over the Chilkoot Pass. Most people begin the hike outside Skagway at Dyea, Alaska, and end at the train station in Bennett, British Columbia. The White Pass and Yukon Route railway transports hikers back to Skagway. Since the trail crosses the border between Canada and the United States, it is cooperatively managed by Parks Canada and the U.S. National Park Service.

## Skyline Trail, AB

The 44.1-kilometre Skyline Trail is quite possibly the most scenic trail in Jasper National Park. Almost 25 kilometres

⬆ **The reward for tackling the challenging Chilkoot Trail is its breathtaking views.**

↑ **Along the Boreal Trail, backpackers can experience the pristine wilderness of northwestern Saskatchewan.**

of the trail is above the treeline, and the high elevation in the Canadian Rockies provides amazing views of craggy mountain peaks, windswept ridges and lush meadows. The trail crosses three mountain passes and can only be hiked between July 1 and October 1. Even then, some parts of the trail can be snow-covered and impassable. Most hikers reserve well in advance and take two to four days to complete the hike — depending on how much time they want to spend exploring the high alpine.

## Boreal Trail, SK

Stretching 120 kilometres, the Boreal Trail allows hikers to experience the beauty of the boreal forest in Meadow Lake Provincial Park. Saskatchewan's only destination backpacking trail leads hikers through stands of spruce and pine, over aspen-covered bluffs and past sparkling, clear lakes. The hike has several start and end points, and the trail can be used for day hiking or multi-day backpacking adventures. Hikers should keep an eye out for birds, black bears and moose as they make their way through the boreal forest.

## Mantario Trail, MB/ON

This 60-kilometre trail in Whiteshell Provincial Park (pp. 92–93) is the longest trail in the Canadian Shield region. Part of the trail passes through the Mantario wilderness zone, an area that is protected from motorized access, hunting, resource extraction and development. Backpackers can explore beautiful lakes and lush boreal forests while traversing hills, bogs, ravines and granite outcrops. White-tailed deer, moose, black bears, minks, beavers, otters and a wide variety of birds may also be seen.

## The Bruce Trail, ON

Southern Ontario's Bruce Trail is the oldest and longest marked hiking trail in Canada. Stretching from the Niagara River to the tip of Tobermory, the trail covers an incredible 890 kilometres of the Niagara Escarpment, a UNESCO World Biosphere Reserve. Hikers can enjoy old-growth forests, badlands, rivers, streams, waterfalls, birds and other wildlife on day hikes or multi-day hikes along sections of the trail. There are campgrounds along the trail, but you may have to book a hotel or B&B for some sections. Besides the main trail, there

↑ The section of the Bruce Trail close to Tobermory features soaring viewpoints overlooking Georgian Bay.

↑ **Backpackers can trek to the intriguing Pingualuk Lake on all-inclusive expeditions in the summer.**

are more than 400 kilometres of side trails, including one that leads to Niagara Falls.

### Pingualuit Crater, QC

The Parc national des Pingualuit is a provincial park in Nunavik, a region that comprises the top third of Quebec and sits above the 55th parallel. It's about as off-the-beaten path as it gets, and exploring this region is only possible on a guided, all-inclusive nine-day trekking tour with Nunavik Parks. Led by local Inuit guides, the multi-day adventure includes hikes around the circular, water-filled and impossibly blue crater known as Pingualuk Lake. The crater

was formed when a massive meteorite crashed into Earth 1.4 million years ago.

### Fundy Footpath, NB

The 41-kilometre Fundy Footpath extends from the Fundy Trail Parkway Visitor Centre in St. Martins, New Brunswick, to the edge of Fundy National Park. This challenging trail leads hikers along the jagged cliffs and mixed forests of the Bay of Fundy, which is home to the world's highest tides. The rugged trail and primitive campsites are maintained by volunteers. Most people take three to four days to hike this trail, and for safety

reasons, all hikers must register at the visitor centre.

## Cape Chignecto Coastal Loop, NS

This challenging 55-kilometre coastal loop wilderness trail at Cape Chignecto Provincial Park will take most backpackers two or three nights to complete. The trail traverses towering 180-metre-high sea cliffs that rise above the Bay of Fundy, which is home to the world's highest tides. It's important to note tide times when exploring this trail. From mid-May to mid-October, hikers enjoy amazing views of pristine coastline, beautiful seasonal wildflowers, rare plants and remnant old-growth forests.

## East Coast Trail, NL

Newfoundland's East Coast Trail spans 300 kilometres along North America's easternmost coastline, from Portugal Cove to Cape St. Francis and on to Cappahayden. A total of 26 wilderness paths make up the trail, which passes through more than 30 historic communities along towering cliffs and past lighthouses, ecological reserves and national historic sites. Hikers may see whales, icebergs, seabirds and the world's southernmost caribou herd as they travel the pathway. Reservations are not required, but donations are appreciated. There are several designated campsites along the trail, and hikers can also stay in B&Bs or hotels.

↑ **Hikers explore the East Coast Trail outside St. John's, Newfoundland.**

# Best Multi-Day Cycling Trails

PIEDMONT 7km

SAINTE-AGATHE-DES-MONTS 35km

MONT-LAURIER 187km

## Kettle Valley Rail Trail/ Columbia and Western Rail Trail, BC

The Kettle Valley Rail Trail and the adjacent Columbia and Western Rail Trail extend from Hope to Castlegar in the longest rail trail network in British Columbia. There are almost 650 kilometres of connected pathways to explore, and the Myra Canyon trestle bridges near Kelowna are a definite highlight.

## Le P'tit Train du Nord Linear Park, QC

Located in the Laurentian Mountains, north of Montreal, this 232-kilometre cycle path is the longest linear park of its kind in Canada. It was built over an old railway line from Bois-des-Filion to Mont-Laurier. The trail can be cycled over multiple days while staying in B&Bs. In winter, the trail is used for cross-country skiing and snowmobiling.

## Petit Témis Interprovincial Linear Park, QC/NB

The first interprovincial cycling network in Canada links the cities of Edmundston, New Brunswick, and

Rivière-du-Loup, Quebec. The picturesque 130-kilometre trail leads cyclists along the shores of the Madawaska River, Lake Témiscouata and the St. Lawrence River.

## Annapolis Valley Trail, NS

This 200-kilometre trail was built on an abandoned rail line and extends from Kentville to Norwood to Yarmouth. In all, there are 21 named sections of trail, which can be used for day cycling or multi-day trips.

## Confederation Trail, PE

Cycle Prince Edward Island from tip to tip on this flat, 435-kilometre rolled stone dust trail. Built on a former railway line, the trail passes through quaint communities that offer a variety of accommodations, restaurants and other services.

↑ **The Confederation Trail is a great way to experience the peaceful scenery of Prince Edward Island's countryside.**

← **Cyclists enjoy the P'tit Train du Nord cycling path near Piedmont, Quebec.**

# Best Aurora-Viewing Spots

The colourful dancing lights of an aurora are created when charged particles from the sun become trapped in the Earth's magnetic field. This happens most often near the magnetic poles. The phenomenon is called aurora borealis at the North Pole and aurora australis at the South Pole. Canada's northern latitude and low light pollution make it an ideal place for viewing aurora borealis. It should be noted that even the best aurora viewing destinations do not see an aurora every night. Conditions have to be right for the aurora to be visible. For example, auroras are less visible during a full moon and not visible at all when skies are cloudy. It's best to plan to be in a destination for several days to increase your chances of witnessing auroral activity. Several spectacular aurora-viewing hot spots have already been mentioned in this book, including Wood Buffalo National Park (pp. 196–97), Jasper National Park (pp. 56–59) and Churchill (pp. 200–203). Here are a few more places where you can witness this awe-inspiring phenomenon.

## Muncho Lake Provincial Park, BC

It's a spectacular site when the northern lights reflect off the glassy, clear waters of Muncho Lake in northern British Columbia. Not far from the Yukon border, this 12-kilometre-long lake is one of the highlights of the Alaska Highway. The lake is surrounded by mountains, so there's great hiking in the area. If you like watching the aurora dance from the comfort of a hot spring, just a few minutes down the road is Liard River Hot Springs Provincial Park. Mid-August to mid-April is peak season for aurora viewing here.

## Fort McMurray, AB

Situated on the 56th parallel, the aurora dances in the skies above Fort McMurray on cold, clear evenings from October through March and occasionally during other months. The aurora is typically seen around midnight, but it can appear any time between 9 p.m. and 3 a.m., lasting for hours or mere minutes. There are tour operators that offer aurora-viewing tours from Fort McMurray.

↑ **The light pollution from Fort McMurray can affect your aurora-viewing experience, so head a few minutes out of town for better views.**

← **Aurora borealis can be viewed across Canada, including here in Lacombe, Alberta.**

↑ The frequency of auroral activity and the relative flatness of the landscape makes Melfort one of the best places in Saskatchewan to view the northern lights, as this photo taken just north of Melfort demonstrates.

## Melfort, SK

About 280 kilometres north of Regina, Melfort has been called "the city of the northern lights" due to the frequency of auroral activity in the area. Spruce Haven Park is a good spot for aurora viewing inside Melfort. If you want to view the aurora while camping, head two hours northwest to Prince Albert National Park (pp. 86–89). The marketing slogan for the province of Saskatchewan is "land of the living skies," and northern Saskatchewan in particular lives up to that reputation.

## The Pas, MB

January to March is peak viewing time for the aurora borealis in most of Manitoba, but in the northern region the dancing lights can be seen up to 300 nights a year. At The Pas, which has been called "the gateway to the north," the northern lights are said to be visible year-round when the skies are clear. The Pas is an isolated group of communities located at the confluence of two rivers about 630 kilometres northwest of Winnipeg.

## Manitoulin Island, ON

At 2,766 square kilometres, Manitoulin Island in Lake Huron is the largest freshwater island in the world. There are more than 100 inland lakes on the island, and above it are some of the darkest skies in Ontario. Gordon's Park is Canada's first commercial dark sky preserve and a great place from which to view the northern lights. Spring and fall are the best times for aurora viewing, and the park hosts aurora borealis–themed weekends.

## Nunavik, QC

Northern Quebec's Nunavik region is an aurora-watching hot spot. The Inuit village of Kuujjuaq is the largest community in this region, with a population of approximately 2,800. The tourism company Inuit Adventures offers multi-day aurora-viewing tours that include airfare from Montreal. During the day, guests experience Inuit culture, visit archeological sites and observe wildlife. Aurora tours run from mid-September through the end of April.

↑ **The sunsets on Manitoulin Island can be as mesmerizing as the northern lights that follow them.**

↑ Tour companies transport you to comfy aurora-viewing posts just outside Whitehorse, which are complete with teepees and yurts.

## Happy Valley-Goosebay, NL

They say the best place to view the aurora borealis in Happy Valley-Goosebay is from the top of OMG Hill at the Birch Brook Nordic Ski Club. Peak viewing time in this region of central Labrador is November through March. Even though the town is Labrador's largest community, with a population of 8,100 people, there is very little light pollution, and the dark skies provide excellent northern lights viewing.

## Whitehorse, YT

The Yukon is legendary for its reliable northern lights displays, and auroras can be spotted throughout the territory. Mid-August to mid-April is the peak season, and dark clear skies provide the best aurora viewing. From Whitehorse, take a drive toward Fish Lake or Chadburn Lake Road to get away from light pollution. There are many companies that offer aurora-viewing tours from Whitehorse. On such tours, guests are bussed outside the city, where there are heated yurts set up, so they can relax and wait in comfort until the aurora comes out. The magic window is typically between 10 p.m. and 3 a.m.

## Yellowknife, NT

The capital of the Northwest Territories is one of the best places in North America for northern lights viewing. The flat landscape along the shores of Great Slave Lake provides unobstructed views, and the low precipitation results in an abundance of cloudless skies. There are many tour operators that offer aurora-viewing tours, and there's even an "aurora village" with heated tee-pees, excellent viewing areas and room to accommodate up to 400 people. Mid-November to the beginning of April is peak aurora season here.

## Iqaluit, NU

There's something magical about the dancing lights of the aurora borealis. One Inuit traditional story relates that the lights are ancestral spirits playing ball with the skull of a walrus. Nunavut, Canada's youngest territory, is an excellent place for aurora viewing. Aurora activity is most visible during the coldest months of the year, but spring and autumn provide good aurora activity with much milder temperatures, which allow for more comfortable viewing. Several tour operators offer aurora tours from Iqaluit.

↑ **Iqaluit is Nunavut's most accessible aurora-viewing spot and a great starting point for further explorations of the territory.**

# Most Scenic Drives

↑ **The Sea to Sky Highway winds along the coast past Stawamus Chief, near Squamish.**

When it comes to road trips, it really is all about the journey. Canada was made for road trips — if you threw a dart at a wall map, marking a random destination, you would find something to love along the way. But for those who like to plan ahead and experience the best of the best, here are some of the most scenic drives Canada has to offer.

## Sea to Sky Highway, BC

What's in a name? In this case, everything. The Sea to Sky Highway from Vancouver to Whistler and Pemberton is filled with remarkable coastal vistas and stunning mountain scenery. It's possible to do the drive straight through, but why would you? This journey needs to be savoured. Stop at a roadside pullout and look for orcas breaching near

↑ The Icefields Parkway traces along many glacial lakes, including Bow Lake.

Vancouver's North Shore. Watch for climbers scaling the 702-metre face of Stawamus Chief near Squamish. Be amazed by the beauty of Howe Sound's steep fjords or the pastoral loveliness of the Pemberton Valley. From start to finish, this is an incredible journey.

## Icefields Parkway, AB

This 232-kilometre stretch of road between Jasper and Lake Louise (also known as Highway 93) was built along the backbone of the North American continent. Interspersed with mountains, glaciers, waterfalls and stunning blue lakes, this roadway has been described as one of the world's most awe-inspiring trips by *National Geographic*, *Condé Nast Traveler* and many other publications. The drive can be done in three hours, but it's best to budget a full day. The Columbia Icefields, for which the road is named, is the largest icefield in the Canadian Rockies, and a stop at Columbia Icefields Discovery Centre is a must. Peyto Lake, Bow Lake, Athabasca Falls, Athabasca Glacier, Sunwapta Falls and Mistaya Canyon are just a few of the other amazing stops that can be made along the way.

↑ **Autumn drives simply don't get any better than along the Algonquin Parkway Corridor.**

## King's Highway 60/ Algonquin Parkway Corridor, ON

Highway 60 is one of Ontario's most scenic highways, leading from Huntsville to Renfrew through Algonquin Provincial Park (pp. 126–29). The road dates to the late 1930s, and though it is beautiful in every season, it is particularly stunning in autumn, when the leaves of the sugar maples and red maples change colour. The 56-kilometre section of road through Algonquin Provincial Park is lined with dense forests, lakes and rivers that can be accessed on foot or in a canoe. It's quite common to see moose and deer along this highway.

## The King's Road, QC

The King's Road, between Montreal and Quebec City, was one of North America's first major driving routes. First opened to traffic in 1737, this 260-kilometre roadway is set along the shores of the St. Lawrence River and has stunning panoramic viewpoints. The road passes though picturesque villages, towns and cities. A journey along this route is the perfect combination of heritage sites, culture and nature. The King's Road is part of Quebec's Route Verte, or Green Route, which means it is safe for cyclists.

## Fundy Coastal Drive, NB

On the 460-kilometre Fundy Coastal Drive, you'll pass half the lighthouses in New Brunswick. You'll also take in the many wonders of the Bay of Fundy, which is home to the world's highest tides. The roadway hugs the southern coast of New Brunswick and passes through colourful maritime communities. Key natural attractions include the Hopewell Rocks, Cape Enrage, Fundy National Park, New River Beach Provincial Park and the Fundy Isles. Keep an eye out for whales in the Bay of Fundy.

## Cabot Trail, NS

The Cabot Trail makes a 297-kilometre loop around Cape Breton Island, and no matter which direction you drive, it's beautiful. There are magnificent coastal views, quaint fishing villages, rivers, valleys, waterfalls, mountains and forests to see and explore. The road passes through Cape Breton Highlands National Park, which is famed for its magnificent fall foliage. Autumn visitors can also attend one of Cape Breton's biggest music festivals, Celtic Colours. Plan to spend a few days so you can hike some of the wonderful trails, feast on seafood and explore the charming communities.

↑ **It's worth pulling over to savour the coastal views along the Cabot Trail.**

↑ **L'Anse aux Meadows National Historic Site is an essential stop along the Viking Trail.**

## Central Coastal Drive, PE

This 253-kilometre coastal drive can be broken into two different touring routes — Green Gables Shore and Red Sands Shore. Green Gables Shore leads you through beautiful Prince Edward Island National Park (pp. 176–77) to the Cavendish region, which was the home of Lucy Maud Montgomery and the setting for her *Anne of Green Gables* novels. Even though there are a lot of commercial tourist sites, there's still unspoiled beauty in the form of red sandstone cliffs, white sand beaches and rolling farm fields. Travelling south along the quieter Red Sands Shore, you'll find red sand beaches and red cliffs to explore.

## Viking Trail, NL

The 489-kilometre Viking Trail begins at Deer Lake and winds along the rugged western coast of Newfoundland. The road goes through quaint fishing villages, UNESCO-recognized Gros Morne National Park (pp. 178–79), the town of St. Anthony and on to L'Anse aux Meadows National Historic Site, the only known Viking settlement in North America. It's a beautiful multi-day drive filled with raw natural beauty. Travellers should keep an eye out for whales and icebergs along the way.

## Dempster Highway, YT/NT

If you like going way off the beaten track, then you'll love the Dempster Highway. The 740-kilometre unpaved road starts near Dawson City and ends in Inuvik, Northwest Territories. Along the way, it passes through magnificent scenery that includes every-thing from mountains to tundra. Wildlife is abundant but services are not, so you should only tackle this drive in a four-wheel-drive vehicle that is in tip-top shape. Even then, you'll need to bring a spare tire and plenty of food, water and fuel. If you want to get a feel for the road without going the full distance, do the stretch from Dawson City to Tombstone Territorial Park. The return trip will take about 3.5 hours.

## Inuvik-Tuktoyaktuk Highway, NT

Opened in late 2017, this is Canada's only all-weather road to the Arctic Ocean, and that alone makes it a cool road trip. The 138-kilometre two-lane gravel highway connects Inuvik with Tuktoyaktuk, a small coastal community on the Arctic Ocean. Previously, the community could only be accessed by an ice road in winter and by plane or boat in summer. The road passes close to the winter grazing grounds of Canada's only reindeer herd. Exploring the two commu-nities provides insight into the culture of the Inuvialuit, who are the western Can-adian Inuit people who live in this region of the Arctic.

↑ **The Dempster Highway allows day trippers to experience the beauty of Tombstone Territorial Park.**

# Best Wildlife-Viewing Spots

↑ **Orcas are spotted in Telegraph Cove, off the coast of Vancouver Island.**

Canada is home to some of the world's most epic wildlife adventures. The world's second-largest country by land mass, Canada is bordered by three oceans and has the world's longest coastline, at 243,042 kilometres. With all that space and so few people, most of the country is wild. Whether your dream is to see polar bears in the Arctic, spirit bears in the temperate rainforest or pronghorns on the Prairies, you can live that fantasy in Canada. Many nature hot spots previously listed in this book are phenomenal for wildlife viewing. Of note are Churchill (pp. 200–203) for its polar bears and beluga whales; Wood Buffalo National Park (pp. 196–97) for its wood bison; Grasslands National Park (pp. 72–73) for its pronghorns, bison and black-tailed prairie dogs; Banff and Jasper National Parks (pp. 52–59) for their elk, moose, and grizzly and black bears; and Gwaii Haanas National Park Reserve (pp. 38–39) for spotting humpback whales. Here are some more of Canada's best wildlife-viewing destinations.

## Telegraph Cove, BC

Every summer orcas, also called killer whales, return to the Johnstone Strait and the Queen Charlotte Strait off Vancouver Island. These powerful predators are the largest members of the dolphin family. Whale-watching season runs from May through October, and there are several tour operators that offer boat tours looking for orcas, humpback whales, dolphins and sea lions. Not far from Telegraph Cove, the Robson Bight (Michael Bigg) Ecological Reserve was established in 1982 as an orca sanctuary. The reserve includes 1,248 hectares of marine area and 505 acres of upland buffer zone that is off limits to boat traffic and human recreation.

## Great Bear Rainforest, BC

In the largest coastal temperate rainforest in the world resides an animal so rare it is the stuff of legends. The kermode bear — also called the spirit bear or ghost bear, particularly by local Indigenous Peoples — is a rare species of black bear that appears white because of a double-recessive gene. The Great Bear Rainforest is its home, along with a vast array of wildlife including grizzlies, black bears, wolves and wolverines. Humpback whales and orcas swim in the waters just off the coast.

## Castle Provincial Park and Castle Wildland Provincial Park, AB

Alberta's newest provincial parks protect more than 1,000 square kilometres of mountains and foothills near Pincher Creek. Long considered sacred to local Indigenous Peoples, the area is home to 120 provincially rare plant species, extremely rare butterflies and 59 species of mammals. It's estimated that more than 50 grizzly bears reside in Castle and the adjacent Waterton Lakes National Park (pp. 42–43). You might also see bighorn sheep, mountain goats, mule and white-tailed deer, moose, wolves, martens, lynx, wolverines, fishers, bobcats and cougars.

↑ Catching a glimpse of the rare kermode bear in the Great Bear Rainforest is one of the most thrilling experiences for a nature lover.

Butala. Located in Reno Municipality No. 51 in south-western Saskatchewan, this conservation area provides important habitat for many species. Visitors can see plains bison, pronghorns, mule and white-tailed deer, coyotes, beavers, porcupines and ferruginous hawks. The endangered burrowing owl and swift fox are also found in the conservation area. An interpretive centre is open weekdays from mid-May through September.

## Narcisse Wildlife Management Area, MB

In cold climates, red-sided garter snakes hibernate in large groups during the winter months. One of the largest known snake dens in Canada is 17.6 kilometres north of Narcisse, Manitoba. The four Narcisse snake dens are home to more than 50,000 red-sided garter snakes, which can be seen when they exit and enter the dens en masse in the spring and fall. During the spring mating season, which runs from the end of April through the first few weeks of May, visitors can witness a "mating ball," in which one female is surrounded by as many as 100 males. There are observation platforms next to the dens and a 3-kilometre interpretive trail runs through native grassland and aspen forests.

## DID YOU KNOW?

The pronghorn is the fastest land animal in North America and the second-fastest in the world, after the cheetah. Unlike the cheetah, which can only run at high speed for a short distance, the pronghorn can maintain speeds of 50 to 70 kilometres per hour over long distances.

## Old Man on His Back Prairie Heritage and Conservation Area, SK

Less than 150 years ago, millions of bison roamed Canada's vast prairies. Today, prairie grasslands are one of the world's most endangered ecosystems. The 5,300-hectare Old Man on His Back Prairie and Heritage Conservation Area is a bright spot thanks to the Nature Conservancy of Canada and former land-owners Peter and Sharon

## Pukaskwa National Park, ON

This 1,878-square-kilometre park along the dramatic shoreline of Lake Superior is the only national park in Ontario that is designated a wilderness park. Here, intrepid travellers can observe moose, American black bears, grey wolves, woodland caribou, beavers, otters and lynx. Most sightings occur along trails or in the backcountry. More than 100 species of breeding birds can also be seen in the park. Bald eagles, great blue herons and herring gulls are common, and a small population of reintroduced peregrine falcons might also be observed.

## Saguenay–St. Lawrence Marine Park, QC

From May to October, the Saguenay–St. Lawrence Marine Park is one of the best places in the world to observe whales. Possible whale species to spot include minke whales, fin whales, blue whales, humpback whales and the endangered St. Lawrence beluga whales. They can be seen right from the shore or on guided boat tours that are offered by private tour operators inside the marine park. From mid-June to mid-October, Parks Canada operates two nearby interpretation and observation centres as well as a marine environment discovery centre.

↑ **Whale watchers catch a glimpse of a minke whale in Saguenay– St. Lawrence Marine Park.**

← **Red-sided garter snakes are harmless, but the sight of 50,000 of them in Narcisse Wildlife Management Area might get your skin crawling.**

↑ **Polar bears are common in Torngat Mountains National Park, and so polar bear guards are essential.**

## DID YOU KNOW?

**Scientists recently confirmed the existence of a hybrid whale that was half-narwhal and half-beluga. It died in the 1980s, but DNA analysis of its skull confirmed that this newly identified "narluga whale" is a result of interbreeding between the two species.**

## Torngat Mountains National Park, NL

Torngat Mountains National Park is one of the most spectacular wilderness areas in Canada. Inside its 9,700 square kilometres are towering mountains and rugged coastline with spectacular fjords and unique wildlife. The park is home to tundra-dwelling black bears, Arctic wolves, muskoxen, wolverines, polar bears and one of the world's largest migratory caribou herds. Guided tours to view caribou and Arctic wolves can be arranged in advance through Torngat Mountains Base Camp. The base camp is open from mid-July to the end of August. Note that visitors need to engage the services of a trained Inuit polar bear guard when hiking or viewing wildlife in this park.

## Pond Inlet and Arctic Bay, NU

The Holy Grail of whale watching is the elusive narwhal. Narwhals have two teeth, and males typically have one tooth that grows very long and appears as a sword-like tusk projecting through its upper lip. The more prominent tooth can measure up to 2.7 metres long. These magnificent animals are found in Arctic waters around Canada, Russia and Greenland. In Canada, Pond Inlet and Arctic Bay are two of the best spots to see narwhals during the summer months. There are several tour companies that

operate in and around Pond Inlet and one in Arctic Bay. It's an expensive trip, but it's worth it if you get to see the legendary unicorns of the sea.

## Ovayok Territorial Park, NU

The muskox is a living remnant of the last ice age. Ancestors of present-day muskoxen roamed the tundra with woolly mammoths and other large mammals that are now extinct. It is the largest Arctic land mammal alive today (polar bears are classified as marine mammals), and Canada is home to the largest naturally occurring muskox population in the world. Most of Canada's approximately 85,000 muskoxen are found on Banks and Victoria Islands in

Nunavut. Ovayok Territorial Park has a resident population that stays year-round, making it a good place to see these ancient creatures. The park is just outside the community of Cambridge Bay, and it is accessible via direct flights to Cambridge Bay from Yellowknife.

↑ Ovayok Territorial Park's muskoxen are a banner attraction to the park.

↖ It is estimated that about 75 per cent of the world's population of narwhals spend their summers in the Canadian Arctic, with many summering near Pond Inlet and Arctic Bay.

# Best Birding Spots

C anada is a birding paradise. Almost 9 per cent of the country (891,163 square kilometres) is covered with fresh water. There are vast tracks of wilderness that include many different ecosystems. Forests, mountains, prairies, lakes, marshes and coastline provide habitat for millions of migrating birds and resident species. Whether you are a Sunday birdwatcher or a seasoned twitcher, there are plenty of amazing birding destinations in Canada. Many of the nature hot spots previously mentioned in this book offer incredible birding opportunities. Of particular note are Point Pelee National Park (pp. 106–7), Long Point Provincial Park (pp. 108–9), the Niagara River (pp. 110–11), Riding Mountain National Park (pp. 96–99), Lesser Slave Lake (pp. 66–67), Grand Manan Archipelago (pp. 160–61) and Bonaventure Island and Percé Rock (pp. 152–53).

## George C. Reifel Migratory Bird Sanctuary, BC

This federal migratory bird sanctuary is 25 kilometres south of Vancouver. It contains nearly 300 hectares of managed wetlands, natural marshes and low dykes in the heart of the Fraser River Estuary and is one of Canada's top birdwatching sites. Nearly 300 species have been spotted here. October and November are particularly good months to visit, as up to 80,000 lesser snow geese turn the sky and land white when they arrive at the sanctuary after a 5,000-kilometre migration from Russia. The organization Birding BC is a good resource for birding in British Columbia, as it provides rare bird alerts, a discussion forum, checklists and information.

## DID YOU KNOW?

In 2016 the Royal Canadian Geographical Society named the Canada jay Canada's official bird. Formerly named the grey jay and often called the "whiskey-jack," it is a hearty bird that can be found in every province and territory.

## Lois Hole Centennial Provincial Park, AB

This globally significant Important Bird Area is only 24 kilometres northeast of Alberta's capital city, Edmonton. More than 220 bird species have been sighted inside the nearly 1,800 hectares of protected area that surrounds Big Lake. Notable species include American avocets, black terns, dowitchers, eared grebes, Franklin's gulls, loons, northern pintails, pectoral sandpipers, tundra and trumpeter swans, and yellowlegs. Osprey and great blue heron can also be seen sometimes. The lake serves as a staging area for migrating waterfowl, and as many as 20,000 tundra swans have been seen in the fall from the boardwalk and viewing platforms.

## Quill Lakes, SK

Recognized as Saskatchewan's first Important Bird Area, these shallow saltwater lakes near Wynard host more than a million visiting birds every year. Over 300 species have been sighted in and around Big Quill Lake, Mud Lake and Little Quill Lake, and the viewing is particularly good during spring and fall migrations. The site is an important staging and breeding area for the endangered piping plover. Other notable species include a variety of shorebirds, ducks, Canada geese, snow geese, American avocets, black-crowned night-herons, great blue herons, great egrets, American white pelicans, Hudsonian godwits, red knots, semipalmated sandpipers, red-necked phalaropes, stilt sandpipers, white-rumped sandpipers and eared grebes.

↑ You can spot both great blue herons and great egrets in the Quill Lakes area.

← This stunning ruddy duck is one of hundreds of species of birds to discover at Lois Hole Centennial Provincial Park.

### DID YOU KNOW?

Every spring and fall, hundreds of golden eagles migrate between wintering grounds and breeding grounds along the same flyway year after year through the Canadian Rockies.

↑ **The sought-after great grey owl is one of the reasons birders follow the Pine to Prairie International Birding Trail.**

## Pine to Prairie International Birding Trail, MB

There are 23 designated stops on this nearly 500-kilometre birding trail, which is an extension of the International Pine to Prairie Birding Trail south of the border, in Minnesota. The route includes several major nature and wildlife areas, including Oak Hammock Marsh (pp. 94–95), Whiteshell Provincial Park (pp. 92–93) and Hecla/Grindstone Provincial Park. This birding trail is a good place to see the official bird of Manitoba, the great grey owl. The endangered piping plover can also be seen from mid-May to mid-August at two stops on the trail. Other sought-after species include Connecticut warblers, spruce grouse, yellow rails, black-backed woodpeckers and Blackburnian warblers.

## Long Point Bird Observatory, ON

Located just outside Long Point Provincial Park, this facility is the oldest bird observatory in the western hemisphere. It was established in 1960 by the Ontario Bird Banding Association and operates research, training and education programs focused on ornithology, conservation and other aspects of natural history. Visit the Old Cut Research Station and Visitor Centre during the spring migration (April to mid-June) and fall migration (early August to mid-November) to watch bird banding demos and enjoy informal tours of

the banding lab and woodlot. More than 400 bird species have been observed in the area, and the bird observatory is one of 17 stops on the South Coast Birding Trail.

## Cap Tourmente National Wildlife Area, QC

This protected area near Quebec's capital region is the first North American site to be recognized under the Ramsar Convention as a wetland of international significance. Inside its nearly 24 square kilometres is critical habitat for the greater snow goose. Flocks numbering in the tens of thousands stop at this site during their spring and fall migrations. Along the 20-kilometre-long network of trails, visitors may observe as many as 180 different bird species, 30 mammal species, 22 types of forest stands and 700 plant species. There are 20 different duck and goose species, 30 warbler species and 10 species of birds of prey, including the peregrine falcon.

## Shepody National Wildlife Area, NB

During early August, semi-palmated sandpipers gather in the hundreds of thousands on the intertidal mudflats and gravel beaches of Mary's Point and Shepody Bay, which are recognized as a Wetland

↑ Dizzying flocks of greater snow geese stop at Cap Tourmente National Wildlife Area in the spring and fall.

↑ **The Shepody National Wildlife Area is a critical stopover for shorebirds like semipalmated pipers, as they make their way to their wintering grounds in Central and South America.**

## Southern Bight-Minas Basin National Wildlife Area, NS

This area at the head of the Bay of Fundy near Wolfville has been designated a Hemispheric Shorebird Reserve and Wetlands of International Importance. The site is composed of intertidal mud flats divided by river channels, and it is an important staging grounds for an estimated 1 to 2 million shorebirds in late July and early August. Commonly observed species include semipalmated sandpipers, black-bellied plovers, red knots, sanderlings, short-billed dowitchers and least sandpipers.

of International Importance, a Site of Hemispheric Importance and an Important Bird Area. Other shorebirds commonly seen include black-bellied plovers, semipalmated plovers, least sandpipers and sanderlings. Peregrine falcons and merlins are often attracted by the shorebirds. Visitors can learn about the birdlife at the Shorebird Discovery Centre. Germantown Marsh is another highlight of the area. The wetlands provide habitat for waterfowl, including American black ducks, green-winged teals, blue-winged teals, ring-necked ducks, American bitterns, pied-billed grebes, soras and others.

## Malpeque Bay, PE

This shallow bay on the north shores of western-central PEI is so big that three provincial parks (Belmont, Cabot Beach and Green Park) lie within it. Recognized as a globally significant Important Bird Area, it contains a variety of bird-friendly habitats, including at least three piping plover beaches. Large numbers of waterfowl are found here, and it's an important staging area for migratory birds. Ram Island has one of the largest colonies of double-crested cormorants in North America. Thousands of Canada geese utilize the bay as a staging area during spring and fall

migrations. Other waterfowl species include red-breasted mergansers, greater scaups, American black ducks and green-winged teals. Shorebirds to look for during fall migrations include greater yellowlegs, willets, whimbrels and red knots.

## Cape St. Mary's Ecological Reserve, NL

The most accessible seabird rookery in North America is a bird-lover's paradise. During the breeding season, Cape St. Mary's is home to 24,000 northern gannets, 20,000 black-legged kittiwakes, 20,000 common murres and 2,000 thick-billed murres. Razorbills, black guillemots, double-crested and great cormorants, and northern fulmars also nest at the site. Walking trails allow visitors to get close-up views of the birds. There are also many species that winter at the site. The reserve can be visited year-round, but the interpretation centre is only open from May until October. Staff at the centre offer guided tours through the reserve and answer questions. Cape St. Mary's is about 200 kilometres southwest of St. John's. Call ahead to confirm weather conditions before heading out.

⬆ **Bird Rock, in Cape St. Mary's Ecological Reserve, is North America's third-largest nesting site for northern gannets.**

# Unusual Nature Hot Spots

↑ **Spotted Lake is known to the Indigenous People of the Osoyoos area as Kliluk and can only be admired from the highway.**

If you want to see something out of the ordinary, Canada is a good place to visit. There are plenty of weird and wonderful natural attractions to explore, but the ones that follow stand out for their quirkiness.

## Spotted Lake, BC

This small, mineral-rich lake is well named: It is covered in colourful spots. The spots develop when water evaporates and leaves behind high concentrations of minerals like calcium, magnesium sulphate and sodium sulphate. The spots shift in size and colour throughout the summer, depending on the level of evaporation. The lake is on private land that belongs to the Okanagan Nation Alliance and has long been revered as a sacred place of healing, but you can see the lake from the highway. Follow Highway 3 west of Osoyoos for 10 kilometres to reach it. Be mindful of traffic when you stop along the highway.

## Abraham Lake, AB

This massive man-made lake in the front ranges of the Canadian Rockies has become "Instafamous" for its ice bubbles. When the sun shines just right, they look like jewels glistening under the surface. When you put the bubbles in the foreground of a picture and the Rocky Mountains in the background, it makes for an incredible composition. But what's the science behind the phenomenon? In winter, pockets of methane gas freeze in layers below the top surface of the ice. The methane gas bubbles are formed as a result of bacteria breaking down organic matter at the bottom of the lake. Bubbles can be found in other Rocky Mountain lakes, but they are typically more visible in Abraham Lake, where strong winds tend to keep the ice surface free of snow. One of the best access points is near the sign for Hoodoo Creek. However, beware of unstable ice in some areas of the lake, where water flows in and out of the Bighorn Dam. Several companies offer ice bubble tours.

## Crooked Bush, SK

There's a great deal of folklore surrounding this 1-hectare stand of mutated trembling aspen trees on private land about an hour's drive northwest of Saskatoon. A short boardwalk trail leads you through a cluster of unusual aspen trees that twist and turn in horizontal and downward directions, giving the grove an eerie appearance. Scientists believe the trees' strange features are the result of a genetic mutation, but they are unsure what caused it. Local legends attribute the bizarre formations to everything from a lightning strike to a UFO landing. It is said that

↑ **The ice bubbles at Abraham Lake enchant nature lovers and photographers alike.**

the years, there have been many reported sightings, and the monster is thought to be anywhere between 3.5 and 15 metres long — depending on which report you believe. Look for the monster while you relax on the beach, fish, swim or go boating on Lake Manitoba. The park is located 55 kilometres north of Sainte Rose du Lac on Highway 276.

↑ A stroll through the Crooked Bush might leave you feeling a bit topsy-turvy.

↗ The Cheltenham Badlands are primarily made of Queenston Shale, which is rich in iron oxide.

→ Fossils at Joggins Fossil Cliffs, like this lycopsid tree fossil, capture what the Earth was like during the Coal Age, over 350 million years ago.

cattle will not travel through the stand of trees, and some people experience feelings of vertigo and dizziness inside the grove. The Redberry Lake Migratory Bird Sanctuary (pp. 84–85) and the Popoff Tree (Saskatchewan's oldest and largest tree) are also nearby.

## Manipogo Provincial Park, MB

A provincial park named after a legendary lake monster is certainly unusual. Local legend has it that the large, serpent-like Manipogo lives in Lake Manitoba. The creature was dubbed Manipogo in 1957, a name similar to British Columbia's fabled Ogopogo lake monster. Over

## Cheltenham Badlands, ON

This unique geological area near Caledon was exposed after soil eroded due to poor agricultural practices during the Great Depression. The colourful badlands landscape unearthed beneath the eroded soil was first formed at the base of an ancient sea more than 400 million years ago, and the beautiful colours are created by iron oxide deposits. This provincially significant area is managed by the Ontario Heritage Trust along with its managing partners, the Credit Valley Conservation and the Bruce Trail Conservancy. There are two formal trails through the badlands — the Bruce Trail and the Badlands Trail, which are connected. You can view the badlands from an accessible boardwalk, but you can't walk on the terrain. There is a parking lot near the boardwalk, and visitors are charged a small fee for using it.

## Magnetic Hill, NB

Drive to the bottom of this hill in Moncton, put your vehicle in neutral, release the brake and see what happens. Not to ruin the surprise, but your car will roll uphill in seeming defiance of gravity. If there happens to be water in the adjacent drainage ditch, it will flow uphill too. Magnetic Hill is Canada's most famous example of a gravity hill, a place where the surrounding landscape creates an optical illusion that makes a slight downhill slope appear to be an uphill slope. At gravity hills, vehicles left in neutral will appear to defy gravity. For a small fee, you can roll up and down the hill as many times as you like.

## Joggins Fossil Cliffs, NS

At this UNESCO World Heritage Site on the shores of the Bay of Fundy, erosion caused by the world's highest tides has uncovered the world's most complete Coal Age fossil record. Nearly 15 kilometres of sea cliffs, bluffs, rock platforms and beach contain a wealth of fossils from the Carboniferous period (354 to 290 million years ago) and the most comprehensive record of the Pennsylvanian strata (dating back 318 to 303 million years). The site is so significant that it has been dubbed the "Coal Age Galapagos" and was cited in Charles Darwin's groundbreaking book The Origin of Species. You can find fossils that predate the first dinosaurs here. Visit the

↑ **Listen for squeaks as you walk along Singing Sands Beach.**

Joggins Fossil Centre to see the exhibits, learn more about fossils and book a guided interpretive tour of the cliffs. The cliffs and the town of Joggins are 222 kilometres northwest of Halifax.

## Singing Sands Beach, PE

When you walk along the beautiful white sand of Singing Sands Beach, or Basin Head Beach, as it is otherwise known, you might hear a squeaking or whistling sound — especially when you shuffle your feet. The phenomenon, which gave the beach its name, is not entirely understood by scientists, but it seems to occur on beaches and desert sand dunes where quartz sand grains are smooth and very

spherical. The noise may be generated by friction between grains of sand or by the compression of air between layers of sand. This lovely beach is in Basin Head Provincial Park, 13 kilometres east of Souris, near the eastern tip of Prince Edward Island. You'll find day-use facilities, including a playground area, boardwalk, gift shop, washrooms and showers.

## Mistaken Point Ecological Reserve, NL

More than 50 ships are known to have wrecked in the perilous waters surrounding the southernmost tip of the Avalon Peninsula, but that's not why it's a UNESCO World Heritage Site. Preserved in the tilted mudstones along this

stretch of rugged Atlantic coastline are the oldest fossils of complex multicellular life found anywhere on Earth. The fossils range in age from 580 to 560 million years, and there are more than 4,000 of them at the site. At the Edge of Avalon Interpretive Centre, you can learn about these important fossils and join a guided hiking tour to take a closer look at them.

## Pingo Canadian Landmark, NT

Some 1,350 pingos, one of the highest concentrations on the planet, can be found in the Mackenzie Delta near Tuktoyaktuk. A pingo is a mound of earth with a core of ice that is found in Arctic and Subarctic regions. Pingos are formed when the pressure of freezing ground water pushes up a layer of frozen earth. These geological formations look very dramatic on the otherwise flat tundra. They can be very large — some reach up to 70 metres high and 600 metres in diameter. The largest pingos take centuries to form, growing a few centimetres each year. The Inuvialuit People have been using pingos as navigational aids for centuries. Just 5 kilometres outside Tuktoyaktuk, the Pingo Canadian Landmark protects eight of these geological features including Ibyuk, the tallest pingo in Canada and the second tallest in the world. The Ibyuk pingo is estimated to be more than 1,000 years old.

↑ **This is one of the eight pingos protected in the Pingo Canadian Landmark.**

# About the Authors

**Debbie Olsen** is a Métis writer and photographer as well as the founder and editor of the popular travel blog *Wander Woman Travel Magazine* (www.wanderwoman.ca). Over her 20-year career as a freelancer, she has won numerous writing and photography awards. Debbie has contributed to 10 Fodor's guidebooks and co-authored the *Globe and Mail* bestselling book *125 Nature Hot Spots in Alberta*. She writes a regular column for the *Calgary Herald* and has written for many other publications, such as BBC Travel, *Westjet Magazine*, *Canadian Geographic*, the *Boston Globe*, *TravelAge West Magazine* and more. She has also appeared on television and radio as an expert guest. Debbie is passionate about nature and the outdoors. In 2012, she was awarded the Queen Elizabeth II Diamond Jubilee Medal in recognition of her significant volunteer contributions toward the connection of the Great Trail (formerly the Trans-Canada Trail).

**Chris Earley (ON)** is the interpretive biologist and education coordinator at The Arboretum at the University of Guelph, Ontario, and a leader for Quest Nature Tours. In addition to authoring *Feed the Birds, Hawks & Owls, Sparrows & Finches* and *Warblers*, Chris co-authored *110 Nature Hot Spots in Ontario*.

**Lyndsay Fraser (BC)** is a bird nerd and insect enthusiast who lives in Courtenay, British Columbia. She is the External Relations Advisor for the Comox Valley Regional District and a science video script writer for the YouTube channel SciShow. Lyndsay co-authored the book *100 Nature Hot Spots in British Columbia*.

**Kyle Horner (ON)** is a naturalist, photographer and educator from Guelph, Ontario. He contributed text and photographs to the book *110 Nature Hot Spots in Ontario*. A birder by trade, Kyle also has a passion for oft-maligned species like snakes and spiders. He has performed field research on both birds and reptiles but has worked primarily as an environmental educator, sharing his excitement for the natural world. Kyle has a degree in Wildlife Biology from the University of Guelph and is the Education Coordinator for Wild Ontario and a birding tour guide for Eagle-Eye Tours.

**Leigh McAdam (AB)** found her way to her home in Calgary after living in Nova Scotia, Ontario, Colorado and British Columbia. She is the author of *Discover Canada — 100 Inspiring Outdoor Adventures*, the co-author of *125 Nature Hot Spots in Alberta* and the creator of the popular blog www.hikebiketravel.com.

**Doug O'Neill (MB)** is an established travel writer who is passionate about nature and the outdoors. He has written for various travel publications, including *Canadian Geographic*, *explore* magazine and *Canadian Traveller*, and co-authored the book *110 Nature Hot Spots in Manitoba and Saskatchewan*.

**Tracy C. Read (ON)** is a Kingston, Ontario, writer and editor and the author of *Wild California*, *Yellowstone* and the children's *Exploring the World of...* natural history series. She is also the co-author of *110 Nature Hot Spots in Ontario*.

**Jenn Smith Nelson (SK)** is an award-winning freelance travel writer and the editor/owner of www.travelandhappiness.com. She co-authored *110 Nature Hot Spots in Manitoba and Saskatchewan* and has contributed to the *Toronto Star*, the *Globe and Mail*, *Canadian Geographic*, *explore* magazine, CBC, Global TV and more.

**Christina Smyth (BC)** is originally from Princeton, British Columbia. Christina co-authored the book *100 Nature Hot Spots in British Columbia* and has worked as an interpretive naturalist and outdoor educator in British Columbia, Alberta and Ontario. She now calls the coastal town of Squamish home, where she works as a secondary school math and science teacher.

# Index

Text in **bold** indicates a photo

# Acknowledgements

I wish to acknowledge the First Nations, Inuit and Métis who have lived on and cared for this land since time immemorial. The enduring presence and stewardship of the Indigenous Peoples of Canada have helped to preserve the many nature hot spots we enjoy today. The land is tied to them and they are tied to the land.

My sincere gratitude to fellow contributors Chris Earley, Lyndsay Fraser, Kyle Horner, Leigh McAdam, Doug O'Neill, Tracy C. Read, Jenn Smith Nelson and Christina Smyth. Their insights, expertise and passion for the outdoors have made *150 Nature Hot Spots in Canada* the special book that it is.

I sought the advice of many experts while selecting, researching, writing and sourcing images for *150 Nature Hot Spots in Canada*. I owe special thanks to Guy Theriault and Eric Magnan with Parks Canada. Sincere thanks to the staffs of many groups and agencies for their assistance and expertise; these include but are not limited to Parks Canada, BC Parks, Alberta Parks, Saskatchewan Parks, Manitoba Parks, Ontario Parks, Quebec's national parks society (Société des établissements de plein air du Québec, or Sépaq), Tourism Quebec, Quebec Maritime Tourism, New Brunswick Parks, Nova Scotia Provincial Parks, Prince Edward Island Provincial Parks, Newfoundland and Labrador Provincial Parks, Newfoundland and Labrador Tourism, Nunavut Territorial Parks and Special Places, Travel Nunavut, Yukon Department of Tourism and Culture and Yukon Territorial Parks. I'd also like to thank the people and organizations that contributed to each of the nature hot spots in this book.

They say a picture is worth a thousand words, but in my experience, it's worth more. A number of photographers contributed stunning images to this book, and I would like to thank all those credited on page 256 for sharing their talents. A special thank you to my husband, Greg Olsen, who contributed many photographs to this book and travelled with me to visit several nature hot spots.

I had many adventures while researching this book. Special thanks to Hilaire Vautour, who kindly assisted me when I was locked out of my Oasis cabin at Kouchibouguac National Park.

A big thanks to the team at Firefly for putting together such a beautiful book. Special thanks to my editor, Julie Takasaki, who spent many hours collaborating and working with me on this project. I am also grateful to Stacey Cho for her design work, Nancy Foran for her careful copyedit and Firefly's editorial director, Steve Cameron, for his ongoing support. A big thanks also to Barry Cuff for his careful proofreading of the manuscript.

And, finally, special thanks to my family who put up with me while I was engrossed in this project and always love me unconditionally. Thanks for all your support.

# Photo Credits

**Alamy Stock Photo**
Alan Dyer/Stocktrek Images: 203;
Alan Dyer/VWPics: 71; Brent Beach:
217; Christopher Price: 234; Cindy
Hopkins: 231; Dianne Leeth: 129;
Don Johnston_PL: 177 (bottom);
Fabrice Simon/Biosphoto: 232;
gary corbett: 243 (bottom); Jordana
Meilleur: 91 (top); Mauro Toccaceli:
93 (top); Megapress: 207 (bottom
left), 214; Mike Grandmaison/
Jaynes Gallery/DanitaDelimont.
com: 101 (top); Rick and Nora
Bowers: 79 (bottom); Skip Moody/
Dembinsky Photo Associates: 100;
Sorin Papuc: 157 (bottom); Stefan
Wackerhagen/imageBROKER: 188;
Timothy Epp: 245; Todd Mintz:
233 (top); Verena Matthew: 215

Alan Watson: 111, 135

Alberta Parks: 48, 63 (bottom), 67, 69

Banff and Lake Louise
Tourism/Paul Zizka: 52, 53

Bonnechere Caves: 124, 125

Bryan Mierau: 81

Chloe Johnson: 31 (top)

Chris Earley: 108, 109
(bottom), 118, 119 (bottom)

Christina Smyth: 16, 17
(bottom), 30, 31 (bottom)

D. Gordon E. Robertson/
Wikimedia Commons/CC
BY-SA 3.0: 139 (bottom)

Dan Strickland: 20

Debbie Olsen: 9, 49, 150, 153,
155, 171 (top), 173, 187 (top),
189 (top), 209, 225, 227

Destination Canada: 97, 99,
200, 201, 202 (top and middle)

Doug Fraser: 12, 13, 18, 19, 26, 35
(bottom), 37 (top), 191 (top), 193

François Guy Thivierge: 149 (bottom)

Frank B. Edwards: 121

Gary Bergen, courtesy of Watrous
Manitou Marketing Group: 80

Greg Olsen: 44, 45, 47 (bottom), 56

Hartley Millson: 104–105,
112, 113, 115, 120

Jenn Smith Nelson: 72, 74 (top), 75,
76, 77 (top and bottom), 78, 89 (top)

John Barnes: 206 (bottom), 216, 241

John Kindrachuk: 85

Kyle Horner: 114, 122, 130, 131 (left)

Leigh McAdam: 43, 54
(bottom), 58 (top), 59, 61, 65

Linda Tholl: 218

Lyndsay Fraser: 14, 37 (bottom)

Manning Park Resort: 25

Mathieu Dupuis, courtesy of
Parc national de Miguasha: 151

Maxine Earl: 235

Meredith Wires: 17 (top)

Michael Murchison: 79 (top)

Municipality of East
Hants: 171 (bottom)

Neil Simon Price, courtesy
of Nunavik Parks: 207
(bottom right), 212

Nick Hawkins/Nature Picture
Library: 181 (bottom)

Oak Hammock Marsh
Interpretive Centre: 94, 95

Ontario Parks: 131 (right),
138, 139 (top), 143

Owen Bjorgan: 133

**Parks Canada**
Brady Yu: 39; Francis Houle: 119
(top); Glen and Rebecca Grambo: 87
(bottom); Greg Huszar: 88 (bottom);
Kevin Hogarth Photography:
87 (top), 88 (top); L. Owen Knox:
73 (bottom); Nigel Fearon: 163
(bottom), 167 (bottom); Parks
Canada: 55; Ryan Bray: 58 (bottom);
Scott Munn: 15, 63 (top), 176, 177
(top); Scott Taylor: 183; Stef Olcen:
10–11, 38; Wayne Lynch: 196, 197

Peter Kelly: 132